PRAISE FOR
THE WEALTH MONEY CAN'T BUY
+ THE AUTHOR
—

"A book of stunning power. If you let it, it'll completely transform your life."
—JEEZY, entertainment mogul and legendary rapper

"A very special book of tremendous usefulness to any human being ready to grow, prosper and lead their lives at the highest level."
—JOHN C. MAXWELL, #1 *New York Times* bestselling author of *The 15 Invaluable Laws of Growth*

"Robin Sharma's work has been deeply helpful to me. *The Wealth Money Can't Buy* is his masterpiece. It's a must read if you want a truly rich life."
—J BALVIN, one of the world's bestselling musical artists

"Robin Sharma has been an amazing mentor to me. He is a major influencer of our time."
—DEEPAK CHOPRA, human potential pioneer and *New York Times* bestselling author of *Abundance*

"Robin Sharma's books are helping people all across the world lead great lives."
—PAULO COELHO, worldwide bestselling author of *The Alchemist*

ALSO BY ROBIN SHARMA

The Everyday Hero Manifesto
The 5AM Club
The Monk Who Sold His Ferrari
The Leader Who Had No Title
The Greatness Guide
The Greatness Guide, Book 2
Who Will Cry When You Die?
Leadership Wisdom from The Monk Who Sold His Ferrari
Family Wisdom from The Monk Who Sold His Ferrari
Discover Your Destiny with The Monk Who Sold His Ferrari
The Secret Letters of The Monk Who Sold His Ferrari
The Mastery Manual
Little Black Book for Stunning Success
The Saint, The Surfer, and The CEO

THE WEALTH MONEY CAN'T BUY

The 8 Hidden Habits
to Live Your Richest Life

Robin Sharma

CROWN
CURRENCY

New York

Copyright © 2024 by Robin Sharma

All rights reserved.

Published in the United States by Crown Currency, an imprint of the Crown Publishing Group, a division of Penguin Random House LLC, New York.
currencybooks.com

CROWN is a registered trademark and Crown Currency and colophon are trademarks of Penguin Random House LLC.

The 5am Club™ and The 4 Interior Empires™ are registered trademarks of Sharma Leadership International Inc.

Simultaneously published in Great Britain by Ebury, an imprint of Penguin Random House Ltd., London, and in Canada by HarperCollins, an imprint of HarperCollins Publishers Ltd., Canada.

Library of Congress Cataloging-in-Publication Data is available with the publisher.

Hardcover ISBN 978-0-593-79849-2
International edition ISBN 978-0-593-79902-4
Ebook ISBN 978-0-593-79850-8

Printed in the United States of America on acid-free paper

Editor: Paul Whitlatch
Editorial assistant: Katie Berry
Production editor: Serena Wang
Production manager: Heather Williamson
Managing editors: Chris Tanigawa & Liza Stepanovich
Publicist: Dyana Messina
Marketer: Kimberley Lew & Julie Cepler

9 8 7 6 5 4 3

Jacket design and art: Pete Garceau

Money is not required to buy any necessity of the soul.
—Henry David Thoreau, philosopher

*Possessions make you rich? I don't have that type of riches.
My riches is life.*
—Bob Marley, legendary reggae musician

The most important things in life are not things at all. Everything I want is right here in front of me. I have wind, I have rain, I have snow, I have sun. So what if I don't have a big home and a big car. I know many people with those things and they still aren't happy.
—Dag Aabye, mountain man and hermit

Contents

A Personal Message from Robin Sharma xv
Introduction xix

THE 1st FORM OF WEALTH
Growth: The Daily Self-Improvement Habit

1. Honor Your Greatness 5
2. Live The Outer Change Follows Inner Change Law 8
3. Don't Be a Resentment Collector 11
4. It's Okay to Be Sloppy 13
5. Memorize The PENAM Principle 15
6. The Best Way to Start Is to Start 18
7. Fears Are Ghost Stories 20
8. Stop Saying These Two Bad Words 22
9. Be The Grown-Up in The Room 24
10. Remember That Small Steps Make Giant Gains 26
11. Worship Your Wounds 29
12. The Human Who Reads The Most, Wins 31
13. Deep Growth Is Meant to Feel Weird 34

14. Expect The Best from People (and You'll Mostly Get It)...... 36
15. Eat Alone Fairly Often 39
16. It's Wise to Keep a Journal 41
17. Your Hurters Are Your Helpers 44
18. Hang with Clowns, Expect a Circus 47
19. Don't Let Self-Care Ruin Your Self-Worth 48
20. Become a Yes Person 50

THE 2ND FORM OF WEALTH
Wellness: The Steadily Optimize Your Health Habit

21. Take a Bath in a Forest 57
22. Know Your Genes Are Not Your Destiny 59
23. The Shortest Chapter in The History of Health Inspiration?... 61
24. See Food as Medicine 62
25. Defend The Health of Your Mind 64
26. Microdose Meditation 67
27. Practice The Naked Sunbathing Rule 69
28. A Sweaty Workout Is Never a Silly Idea 71
29. Do a 30-Day Zero-Sugar Challenge 73
30. Commit to a Dopamine Detox 75
31. Become a Professional Sleeper 77
32. Show Up in The Gym The Way You Wish to Show Up in Life.. 79
33. Become a Skilled Lifetime Multiplier 82
34. Go OMAD Weekly 84
35. Laugh More to Live Longer 86
36. Breathe Like a Samurai 89
37. Chant Like a Monk 90
38. See Solitude as a Wellness Method 92

39. Supersize Your Gratefulness 94
40. Consider That Cold Showers Decrease Doctors 97
41. Exercise Your Spiritual Wellness.. 99

THE 3RD FORM OF WEALTH
Family: The Happy Family, Happy Life Habit

42. That Time My Mother Took on a Motorcycle Gang......... 105
43. Create a Love Account 107
44. Live The Loved Ones' Eyeballs Law 109
45. Savor The Small Surprises of Family Life 110
46. Don't Carry Grudges 111
47. Practice Tough Love 113
48. Your Choice of Mate Is 90 Percent of Your Joy 115
49. Practice The 3 Great Friends Rule 117
50. Record The Ride 118
51. Ask The 10,000 Dinners Question 120
52. Know Opposites Don't Attract 122
53. See Little Children as Giant Gifts...................................... 124
54. Some Hurts Aren't Meant to Be Healed 126
55. Do Not Be a Doormat.. 128
56. Know That Attachment Is Not Love 129
57. Give More Hugs.. 130
58. Turn into a People-Builder 131
59. Be a Perfect Moment Creator... 132
60. A Gift Given to Receive Isn't a Gift 134
61. Other People's Bad Behavior Is Not Your Business 136
62. Listen Better Than You Speak.. 137
63. Remember That Our World Is Your Family 140

THE 4TH FORM OF WEALTH
Craft: The Work as a Platform for Purpose Habit

64. The Good Nun in The Country Church 145
65. Don't Be So Logical You Can't See The Magic 147
66. The You Don't Get Lucky You Make Lucky Maxim 149
67. Start a Stop Doing List... 152
68. Avoid The "No One Will Notice It" Lie 154
69. Bring a Security Guard to Work.................................... 156
70. Use The Virtuoso Algorithm... 157
71. Learning Is Your Superpower 160
72. Develop a Lust for Books 163
73. Live The Grandmaster Beginner Law............................ 165
74. Make Your Project X.. 168
75. Hard Work Is Great Work... 170
76. First Drafts Are Meant to Be Bad.................................. 172
77. Stop Copying Your Heroes 174
78. Just Be Friendly 176
79. Set Your Daily 5 178
80. Think Like an Artist 180
81. Find Your Personal Goldeneye...................................... 182
82. Go The Extra Mile 184
83. Be Patient Like a Pro 186
84. Be Like a Dog with a Bone... 188
85. Enjoy The Time You Waste 190
86. Apply The 60-Second Anti-Procrastination Rule 192
87. While You're Working, Keep Improving....................... 194
88. Labor for The Magic, Never for The Money 196
89. The Michelin–Three Star with The Very Absent Chef ... 198
90. Life Is More Important Than Work.............................. 200

THE 5TH FORM OF WEALTH
Money: The Prosperity as Fuel for Freedom Habit

91. Avoid The Howard Hughes Money Trap 207
92. Know Your Scarcity Scars 209
93. Your Vitality Serves You Financially 213
94. The Top Move of Money Masters 215
95. The Multibillionaire in The Very Empty Mansion 218
96. Grateful Is a Money Printer 221
97. See Another's Winning as Your Victory 223
98. Remember The Habits Beat IQ Slogan 225
99. Use Wealth Words 227
100. Run The Tracey Emin Anti-Cocaine Rule 229
101. Live Beneath Your Means 231
102. The Habit Stack of Super-Wealthy People 234
103. Develop The Doubling Discipline 237
104. Translate Video-Watching into Fortune-Making 239
105. Why Do It if It Doesn't Make You Happy? 241
106. Recruit a Dead Board of Directors 243
107. Sit for Rich Ideas 245
108. Bless Your Money Daily 246
109. Being Good Is Good Business 248
110. Be a Highly Humble Leader 251
111. The Investment with The Highest Return 254
112. Ask The Billion-Dollar Business Question 257
113. Silently Adore Your Haters 259
114. Greedy Is Not Happy 261
115. Go Relational, Not Transactional 262
116. My Top 10 Books for Prosperity 264
117. To Make a Million, Help a Million 265

THE 6TH FORM OF WEALTH
Community: The You Become Your Social Network Habit

118. Choose a Brighter Neighborhood 271
119. Live Your Hero's Life 273
120. Do What You Say You'll Do 274
121. Start a Mastermind Alliance 276
122. The Stephen King Lost Letters Rule 278
123. Karma Is Not Mystical, It's Practical 280
124. Remember The Vanishing Loved Ones Law 282
125. Why Have an Enemy When You Can Make a Friend? 284
126. Be a Major Gift Giver 286
127. Increase Your Charisma 289
128. Go See People in Person 292
129. You Never Know Who Someone Will Become 293
130. Wish People a Great Day 295
131. Talk to Weirdos 297
132. Dig Your Well Before You're Thirsty 298
133. Don't Be a Servant to Your Phone 299
134. Make Others Feel Special 301

THE 7TH FORM OF WEALTH
Adventure: The Joy Comes from Exploring Not Possessing Habit

135. Find Your Invisible Panama 307
136. Watch a Lot of Documentaries 309
137. Take a Digital Sabbatical 310
138. Release The Energy Vampires 312
139. Start a Garden 313

140. Become a Poet.. 315
141. Slow Everything Down 318
142. Go Ghost for a Year... 319
143. Seek The Mysterious in Your Work 321
144. Win The Memory Lottery... 323
145. Do Something Scary Every Three Months 324
146. Pretend You're a Pirate 326
147. Pursue Your Passions... 328
148. Less Mastery, More Mystery 330
149. Stop Salting Your Food Before You Taste It 332
150. Happiness Is an Inside Job.. 334
151. Do a Possessions Purge 335
152. My Top 10 Books on Leading a Life of Astonishment 336
153. Create an Anti-Hero Scenario... 337
154. Avoid The Old Person Flaw.. 339
155. Find Your Metaphorical Wolfgat..................................... 341

THE 8TH FORM OF WEALTH
Service: The Life Is Short So Be Very Helpful Habit

156. Find a Cause That's Bigger Than Yourself...................... 347
157. Put Your Final Day First... 349
158. Memorize Alexander The Great's Last 3 Wishes 351
159. Lead Without a Title... 353
160. Trust The Power of Not Caring 354
161. Your Heart Is Wiser Than Your Head............................. 355
162. Don't Let Another's Bad Day Ruin Yours........................ 357
163. Recite The Just Like Me Peacefulness Prayer.................. 359
164. See Solitude as The New Status Symbol......................... 361
165. Apply The Kindness Always Motto 362

166. Doing a Good Thing Is Never a Bad Thing 363
167. Reflect on The Lost Sovereigns Law 366
168. Remember You Only Need Six Feet 367
169. Start a Love Revolution 370
170. The High Road Is The Best Road 372
171. Eat Your Last Supper Today 375
172. Do Three Anonymous Acts of Goodness 377
173. You Matter Much More Than You Know 379
174. Have a Living Funeral 381
175. Live Fully So You Can Die Empty 383

A Personal Message from Robin Sharma

I'm writing you this note from the farmhouse I live in. Through the window of the room where I do my work, I can see the olive grove, vineyards, and a vast mist floating over the hills that seem to reach for the heavens. It would be good if you were here with me so I could tell you, in person, everything I wish to share about a life richly lived. Maybe we can do this in the future. Let's see.

My sincere wish—as you pass through this book that I have written to help you live the highest version of the greatest vision you have of your life—is that I earn more and more of your trust as the book unfolds. And become your companion, friend, and mentor.

I humbly and honestly thank you for believing in the value of the ideas you are about to discover on leading an existence filled with true success and real wealth rather than the fake version that has been programmed into too many good people. I hope this book that I've worked so hard on will serve you to make a life of far greater beauty and happiness, courage and connection, along with an inner peace that has no bounds.

Please note that my philosophy of what makes a great and glorious human life—on which this work is based—is very different from that of other books in the personal development field. I simply ask you to keep an open mind as we progress through it and measure whether the information is valuable by the actual results it delivers into your days.

Okay. Let us begin.

There's an old story of a young boy who spends his evenings in the countryside watching the sun set over a perfect home on a faraway hill, with windows that appear to be made of gold. He is utterly consumed by the idea of—some time in the future—making the journey to visit this place and hopefully, eventually, living in it. For to do so would give him the happiness he so deeply desires.

One day when he's slightly older, he sets out to make his dream real. He journeys for many days and even long nights, surviving solely on the kindness of strangers who encourage him to keep on walking when they hear of his ambition to visit the perfect home, with windows of pure gold. Eventually, exhausted and spent, the boy arrives at his destination.

Yet of course, it's not at all what he saw it to be. Instead of perfection, the house is a broken-down barn. And rather than the windows being made of perfect gold, they are old, dirty, and cracked. He realizes that, from afar, the barn's position on the lofty hill had created an optical illusion: the lightfall on the windows made them seem fashioned of precious metal. But what he had seen from a distance was a lie.

Oh, what a world we live in! We are trained to measure whether we are winning by the amount of money we have, the size of the possessions we own, and how well we have used our best days in pursuit of fame, fortune, and influence. This causes too many of us, deep within our souls, to feel bad about our lives, sad about ourselves, and mad that the dreams we once had such faith in have been destroyed, dying a quiet death as we replaced them with adult responsibilities, life's stresses, and human struggles.

Sure, money is important. Having a reasonable amount allows us to lead easier lives, live life on our own terms, and do good things for the people we love. Having enough opens more windows of possibility and doorways of choice. Yet money is only one form of wealth—there are actually seven other forms I'd like you to focus on, so we get you to a life that you feel is honestly rich, deeply alive, and everything you once hoped it would be. I'll teach you these, along with a very powerful method, with all the enthusiasm I have, as we move ahead together.

Sometimes we're so busy looking at what others own that we forget all the blessings we have. And I'm not only writing about material things when I say this. I'm writing more about the essential elements of a human life beautifully lived. Ones that are just too easy to neglect in this fast, overly complex, and continuously messy world you and I now find ourselves in. Things that may now seem unimportant yet when you're at your final hour of your last day come into clear focus as being the most important.

One of the reasons I wrote *The Wealth Money Can't Buy* is that so many people—across this planet—are suffering. Suffering from thinking and feeling that they don't have enough. Enough money. Enough material possessions. Enough likes, followers, and social status. This, in turn, causes what I call in my mentoring work The Suffering of Unworthiness. Too many among us have a profound sense that we just don't matter and that we just aren't successful and that our lives are too small, when compared to lives we are told are perfect and big.

Here's the truth: You are absolutely and uniquely and undeniably enough. You have such gifts, talents, and goodness. And so very much to be grateful for, right now. Yet so many have a sort of hole within us. And here's the trap: We push ourselves mercilessly to seek more and more external things to fill that hole. Falsely telling ourselves that when we have overflowing cash and flashy cars and fashionable clothes and online followers, one day, we will magically wake up feeling okay. And lastingly happy. Yet you and I know that day will never come. Because nothing in the outer world will ever make you feel better on the inside. As the Zen proverb confirms: "Wherever you go, there you are."

So what's the solution? Simple: to understand that what you are chasing in this collective pursuit of climbing the popular mountain of success—which society has trained us to climb—will not lead you to real success. Because reaching the summit of money but getting there feeling empty, lonely and unhappy, isn't winning. It's losing. You don't want to be like that young boy in the story I shared who chases an ideal only to learn it was a lie.

"Success occurs in the privacy of the soul," wrote famed music producer Rick Rubin. Worldly success without a joyful heart is fool's gold. My humble prayer is that you experience both. The book you hold in your hands is my gentle offering that will lead you to experience the genuine victories, soaring cheerfulness, and magic—yes, magic—that makes a human life great. I've poured my mind, heart, body, and spirit into this work. I hope it serves your rise marvelously well.

With love and respect,

Introduction

The other night, Elle sat on the sofa next to me, in the living room of our farmhouse in the Italian countryside. We moved here a few years ago, with the most important possessions of my life stuffed into three suitcases. I needed a new adventure, so I sold my home, gave away many of my things, and left the country I'd lived in for fifty-five years. After we landed in Rome, we waited at the baggage carousel, excited by the beginning of our fresh life. Then we waited some more and then a little more. Yes, our luggage was lost. The universe has a hilarious sense of humor, doesn't it?

Anyway, on this evening at the farmhouse that I was just about to describe to you, Elle's little dog, Holly, who has now become my little dog as she's pretty much with me all the time, sat on my lap—sort of purring like a cat (yet she really is a dog). I call Holly "SuperChum," because that's exactly what she is to me.

Looking out the ancient window frames, I saw the sun-setting sky all fiery and enchanting with hues of red and hints of burnt orange. It was magic, in its simplest form. Italy does that to you. A friend recently told me, "You cry twice when you live here. First when you get here, because it's not the most efficient place in the world. And then you cry a second time, whenever you have to leave." Yes, it's that special.

Elle had a soft smile on her face. And sometimes a few tears in her eyes. She was reading the manuscript of this book, for the first time.

The whole scene was super simple. And profoundly perfect.

It made me think these words: "This is rich."

I'm certainly not saying my life is or has ever been ideal. Not at all. I've experienced dramatic difficulties and endured some monumentally hard times. I've been knocked down, kicked around, betrayed, and deeply dismayed.

And I sure don't want you to think that I'm some kind of guru who knows it all. Because I am not.

Yet I have discovered how to turn setbacks into strengths, wounds into wisdom, problems into prosperity. I have earned a lot of hard-won lessons on living beautifully to share with you, in our time together, on the pages ahead.

I once had a ski instructor who helped me ski better (because that's what ski instructors do). While we were riding the ski lift up the mountain one day he said, "You know, ski instructors aren't rich, but we have a rich life." And that man—with always-rosy cheeks from the sunshine and cold, a wife he adored, children he cherished, and a lifetime spent on a mountain with views that left me breathless—was the wealthiest person I've ever known.

This is what *The Wealth Money Can't Buy* is all about: the real riches that often sit right in front of us, but we ignore because we have been programmed not to value them. Makes me think of this quote by Dale Carnegie: "We are all dreaming of some magical rose garden over the horizon instead of enjoying the roses blooming outside our windows today." True, right?

Let me ask you: "Why does our culture worship the billionaire, yet not the teacher who finds a way to inspire a class of twenty children week after week? Or the firefighter whose heroic dedication helps to keep us safe in our communities and homes? Or the gardener who makes the street more marvelous through their tireless efforts to plant, nurture, and water the neighborhood's flowers?"

This book is about a completely new philosophy and methodology of success and wealth that we are not schooled, trained, or even encouraged to consider. But one that will absolutely bring you sustained happiness, personal freedom, and lasting internal peace.

Now, as I've mentioned, I do agree that money is important. We all have bills to pay, obligations to meet, and pursuits to engage in that cost cash. And having strong savings and financial abundance allows you to live with less stress, more freedom, and a sense of personal sovereignty (doing what you want, where you want, when you want—with the people you love). So yes, money is an essential element to your richest life. I must be extremely clear on that. It's something important yet not everything important.

As you'll see in the learning framework I'm about to offer you (one that I've taught to my private advisory clients for many years with excellent results), financial prosperity is only one of the eight forms of wealth. I've mentored many billionaires over my nearly three decades of working with many of the world's business titans, professional sports superstars, film icons, and movement-makers. And I can safely tell you that, for too many of them, money is all they have. They are cash rich yet life poor.

You really need to be doing well in each of the eight forms of wealth to be able to call yourself truly successful and someone who is really living abundantly. And beautifully.

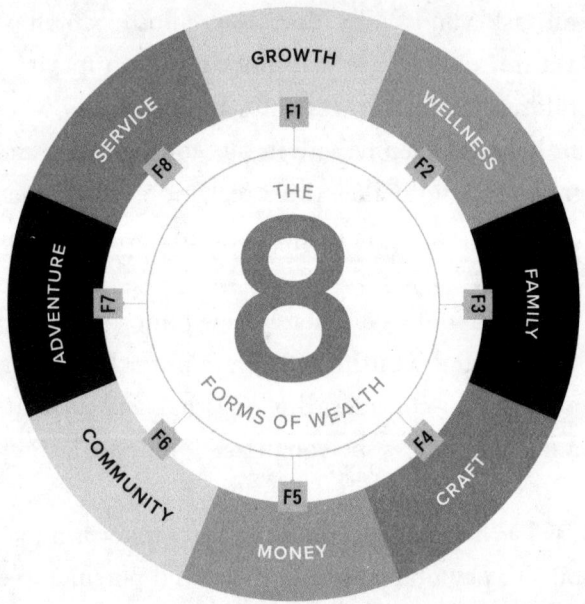

On the pages ahead, we will carefully consider each of the eight forms of wealth shown above, in a way that is easy to apply, fun to understand, and powerful in the difference it will make in your days. In short chapters designed to be personal daily mentoring sessions, I will provide you with ideas, suggestions, instructions, and stories of inspiration so you can more fully live each one of them. And as you do, you will see that you will be rewarded with your richest life.

The 8 Forms of Wealth learning model is based upon eight hidden (because they are not so commonly considered) habits that I energetically urge you to embrace:

Growth: *The Daily Self-Improvement Habit.* This habit is based on the insight that humans are happiest and genuinely wealthiest when we are steadily realizing our personal gifts and primal talents. The regular pursuit of personal growth is one of your most valuable assets.

Wellness: *The Steadily Optimize Your Health Habit.* This habit is founded on your deep understanding that peak mental, emotional, physical, and spiritual vitality and living a long life filled with energy, wellness, and joyfulness are mission-essential to you being honestly rich.

Family: *The Happy Family, Happy Life Habit.* This habit is built on the knowledge that having all the money and material success in the world is worthless if you are all alone. So enrich the connections with the ones you love. And fill your life with fantastic friends who upgrade your happiness.

Craft: *The Work as a Platform for Purpose Habit.* This habit is grounded in the consistent practice of seeing your work as a noble pursuit and an opportunity not only to make more of your genius real, but also to make our world a better place. Mastery is a currency worth investing in.

Money: *The Prosperity as Fuel for Freedom Habit.* This habit is driven by the principle that financial abundance is not only far from evil but also a necessity for living in a way that is generous, fascinating, and original.

Community: *The You Become Your Social Network Habit.* This habit is structured around the scientific fact that a human being's thinking, feeling, behaving, and producing are profoundly influenced by their associations, conversations, and mentors. To lead a great life, fill your circle with great people.

Adventure: *The Joy Comes from Exploring Not Possessing Habit.* This habit is formulated around the reality that what creates vast joy is not material goods but magical moments doing things that flood us with feelings of gratefulness, wonder, and awe. Enrich your days with these and your life will rise into a whole new universe of inspiration.

Service: *The Life Is Short So Be Very Helpful Habit.* This habit is founded on the time-honored understanding that the main aim of a life richly lived is to make the lives of others better. As you lose yourself in a cause that is bigger than you, you will not only find your greatest self but will illuminate the world in the process. And discover treasures far beyond the limits of cash, possessions, and public status.

All right. Thank you again for your faith in my work and for joining me here. Now, let us start. So we fill your days with the wealth money can't buy.

THE 1ST FORM OF WEALTH

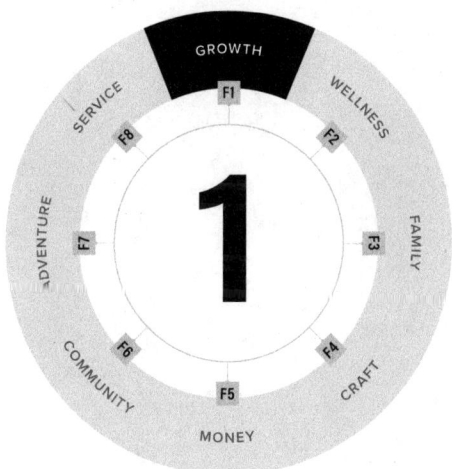

Growth

The Daily Self-Improvement Habit

The wealth within you, your essence,
is your kingdom.
—Rumi

The 1st Form of Wealth
Growth | Quick Overview

To grow into all you can possibly be is a prize far more precious than anything money could ever buy. Personal mastery is a currency that will make you authentically wealthy. And your wisest investment is making yourself into all you can be.

To explore your unfaced fears, to release sabotaging limitations, to venture into the unknown fields of your native potential and to know how wise, strong, gifted, resilient, and loving you are will bring more magic into your life than all the fame, fortune, and worldly success one could ever have.

Inner growth and daily personal development are a very real form of wealth, though our society generally doesn't value them. Instead, in our current age, it's the billionaire financial titan who is placed on the front cover and the famed sports superstar placed on a pedestal instead of the person who has made the making of a pure mind, the building of a rich heart, the construction of a heavyweight character, and the growing of a soaring spirit their primary priority. To me, winning within is so much more important than winning in the world. The first is enduring. The second is fleeting.

Yet just because our culture doesn't put self-improvement and the ongoing realization of your natural powers and primal genius near the top of any list of the things that matter most to a journey well-lived doesn't mean that you shouldn't. You should, actually.

Mahatma Gandhi once said, "The only devils in the world are those running around inside ourselves. This is where the battle should be fought." And please trust me: once you get the value of deepening your personal growth, everything will change for you. Because a brilliant outer life begins with a beautiful interior one. And you will never be able to create, produce, prosper, and savor any higher than what you are.

Okay, my new friend, let's explore the first form of wealth, together.

1

Honor Your Greatness

A simple idea that's too often neglected. To appreciate *you*. For all you've gone through and all you've become. For all the fears you've faced and found freedom from. For the dreams you not only dreamed but had the bravery to make real. For all the people you've helped and for all the good you have done. You matter more than you know. So please do not measure your worthiness by what the majority tells you that you should be, do and have.

You being here with me is no accident, at all. Something in you—in a culture where too many fine people are sleepwalking through their most precious hours in a digital slumber—seeks something higher. I sense that although life can be hard at times, you have not lost your hope. You've protected your optimism for your brighter future and trusted that call within your soul to fully realize your ethical ambitions for all the time you get to live.

This—to my getting-sort-of-old eyes—makes you a hero. You've been through a lot. You could have given up. And become jaded, cynical, critical, and closed-hearted.

Yet, instead, here you are. Ready to rise, passionate to advance and dedicated to grow through the guidance you are receiving through me, as your mentor. It's an act of high courage to be willing to let go of who you were yesterday to become someone even better, wiser, healthier, and happier tomorrow, you know?

Oh, and I really should reinforce that personal development work is the best work you could ever do. A lot of people snicker or roll their eyes (or both) when they hear the term "self-improvement." Yet what is more courageous and sensible than steadily and incrementally doing the deep training to turn everyday human insecurity into rare-air confidence, personal limitation into uncommon prowess, and an average mode of rolling through life into a breathtakingly exceptional journey that honors the promise you have been born into? "The most important investment you can make is in yourself," noted renowned financier Warren Buffett. And the finest strategy to make the world better is to make yourself better, right?

As you rework, elevate and calibrate your inner universe, your relationship with what I call in my mentoring methodology your Heroic Self (which is the opposite of your Egoic Self, the false, faulty, restricted, and scared part of you that has been formed by the negative beliefs and human hurts that you've endured in your past) will definitely increase. And when your primary relationship with your greatest self increases, *every* other relationship in your life increases too.

Build stronger knowledge and intimacy with your Heroic Self (through the philosophies and tools I'll walk you through) and your relationship with your family, vitality, work, prosperity, community, adventure, and service to others will fly with it.

By the way, you should know right now that I come from humble beginnings. No silver spoon in my mouth. Born in Africa. Came from immigrant parents. Two years ago, I took my life partner, Elle, to see the house I grew up in. The current owner was watering the lawn when we walked up to the place. I told him that I used to live in his home, over fifty years ago. So he invited us in. Nice man. Smiled a lot.

After we left, Elle said, "That's the smallest house I've ever seen." I felt the same way.

And I grew up with a ton of flaws—as all humans do. Filled with thoughts of scarcity, emotions of timidity, sensations of insecurity and methods of operating that chained my talents, restrained my optimism, and smothered my freedom.

Yet one thing saved—and transformed—me: a limitless (and sometimes obsessive) love of growth. If I didn't know how to improve something, I could learn how to do it. All I longed to become and everything I dreamed of experiencing could happen by enriching my understanding. Of course, *you can do this too*. Which is why I'm so excited for you.

As I write these words, I am reminded of what the philosopher and writer Ayn Rand wrote:

> Do not let your fire go out, spark by irreplaceable spark in the hopeless swamps of the not-quite, the not-yet, the not-at-all. Do not let the hero in your soul perish in lonely frustration for the life you deserved, but have never been able to reach. The world you desire can be won, it exists, it is real, it's yours.

Such are the wishes that I hold dear for you.

2

Live The Outer Change Follows Inner Change Law

As I write you this mentoring message I do hope you're in great spirits, full of enthusiasm (what a great word that is!), and in hot pursuit of a gorgeous life that you'll be proud of when you're an old-timer. And if you're already an old-timer, then my prayer is that you're already proud of your life.

I was up at three this morning (went to sleep just after 9 PM) so I could meditate, visualize, and pray. Then I hopped onto my elliptical machine. It's my favorite piece of exercise equipment, unless we include my trusted mountain bike. That one's tops for me. When I first met Elle—on our second date, to be accurate—the first thing I showed her when she visited my home was my mountain bike. She later confided that she thought that was a little strange. But all these years later she's still with me. So I guess it was an okay move.

Anyway, I need to share a story. One evening a father sat in his favorite chair, reading a newspaper. His young son sat near him. "Dad, let's play," the boy said cheerfully. But the man was too busy being an adult and kept on studying his paper.

"Daddy, let's play! Let's have fun," the little boy said. Yet the father paid him no attention. He continued his reading.

The child persisted and the man ignored him. Finally, the father had an idea. There was a picture of the globe in the newspaper, so he tore it out, ripped it into dozens of pieces, and handed it to his son, saying, "Here, go put this back together," thinking it would take the child a long time to do it.

Yet children come to us more highly evolved than adults to teach us the lessons we need to learn. And after only a few minutes the boy came back with the globe *perfectly* back together.

"How'd you do that, Son?" the father asked, astonished.

"Easy, Dad. On the other side of the globe was a person. And once I got the person together, the world was okay."

Powerful idea, right? Once you get yourself together, *your* world will be okay—more than okay. Fantastic, actually, *if* you practice the philosophies, methods, routines, and tactics that I'm super excited to share with you (nothing works for someone unwilling to do any work, yes?).

One of the brain tattoos I love sharing with my audiences when I do a keynote presentation in some city across this small planet is this: "Victims make excuses; leaders deliver results." To be a leader doesn't mean you must have a title, a position, authority, or a ton of money. Nope, not at all.

Leadership's just the opposite of victimhood. And human beings giving away their power to create wonderful results by complaining, blaming, and expecting others to make things better for them are people caught in the trap of playing the victim.

The other day I was in a ride-sharing car with a cool young driver. As we chatted, he shared that he arrived as an immigrant with $260 in his pocket. That was all the money he had in his life. Yet, by his focus, hard work, and relentless desire to grow, he saved up enough to buy a house and was now supporting eleven (yes, eleven!) of his family members. He could have complained of his hard past, blamed his mean childhood, and waited for something outside of himself to improve his days. But he didn't. He started small, made steady daily gains, and transformed his situation over time. This ride-share driver delivered results instead of making excuses. And he told me his real secret was his deep dedication to constant self-improvement, which is really all about growth—the first form of wealth.

For some reason this man's story makes me think of the words of the warrior poet Charles Bukowski: "Can you remember who you were, before the world told you who you should be?"

We should end this chapter on that. Because I need a break from writing and my trusty mountain bike is waiting for me.

3

Don't Be a Resentment Collector

Someone looks at us the wrong way. Someone close to us disappoints us. Someone we trusted lies to us. Such things are part of the essence of life. You can't avoid them, much as you try.

When we are not treated as we wish to be treated, it's so easy to get angry. Or to withdraw. Or to harbor a secret resentment.

And as we advance through life and interact with other human beings, it's easy to keep adding to what I call The Resentment Stack.

You just keep getting discouraged, and rather than processing through the emotions of hurt, frustration, and irritation these experiences create so you are free of them, you just swallow them all. And wallow in them. And let the resentments fester, like a great gaping wound (that stains every moment you experience and tarnishes your creativity, productivity, prosperity and serenity).

You're wise and bright, and you pick really great mentors, so you already know: this is not the best way to live. Wounds unhealed become potential unrealized, along with a serious drain on your energy—energy that could be used to create soaring results and to enjoy this supreme gift and expedition that is your life.

And also remember this: the bigger your Resentment Stack grows, the more it colors the way you see *everything*.

You start seeing slights that weren't even there. You begin to perceive people doing mean things that they didn't really do. You begin to believe that this sometimes difficult yet also utterly amazing universe we live in is a very scary place. We see things not as they are but as *we* are, right?

So my sincere suggestion for you, as I sip my fresh mint tea infused with a sliver of ginger and listen to Kolby Cooper's enchanting country music song "Fall," while a very noisy rooster continues to wake up the world, is to become *a master of letting things go*. Sure—of course—protect yourself and stand up for good treatment. That's obvious and we do teach people how to treat us. You must never allow anyone to walk over you. Yet I also carefully suggest that you increase your compassion for others. We don't know what battle they are fighting. And everyone around us really is doing their best. (Even if their best is a mess.)

And while this does not mean they shouldn't be held accountable for the things they do, it does mean they deserve our understanding. Just imagine how bright a human life you'll create if you operate in the rare air of seeking to see the blessings in the people who try to curse you. Such is the behavior of history's greatest souls. And a truly wealthy person.

"In my younger and more vulnerable years my father gave me some advice that I've been turning over in my mind ever since. 'Whenever you feel like criticizing anyone just remember that all the people in this world haven't had the advantages that you've had,'" said Nick Carraway, the narrator in F. Scott Fitzgerald's majestic novel *The Great Gatsby*.

Get this one piece right and your daily joy and overall peacefulness will escalate exponentially. And by the life you lead, you'll subtly prompt peace to break out, all across the planet.

4

It's Okay to Be Sloppy

"Be perfect" and "be super tidy" and "have cut abs," our society schools us. What nonsense!

Is it not a mark of high wisdom to live a richly *balanced* life?

There are times to exercise world-class willpower (while creating an inspiring work project, pursuing an important physical fitness goal, or realizing a meaningful spiritual venture, for example) and model heroic self-discipline. Then there are periods meant for leaning back, resting more, doing little, and simply being a human *being*.

And when I say in the title of this mentoring message that it's okay to be sloppy, in certain seasons of your life's journey, I don't just mean not making your bed when you don't feel like it or keeping your schedule empty so you give yourself the freedom to be bored. I also mean it's okay to be less than perfect when it comes to your inner life. Self-mastery and personal growth must never be a grind. Otherwise, you'll drain the magic out of the entire enterprise.

Last night, I watched an online video of a man saying that we should treat ourselves like a slab of rock, striking ourselves to our most extreme edges to sculpt something beautiful. His energy was intense, aggressive, and seemingly angry.

I get his point. I sure do. We can't constantly give in to weak impulses every hour yet hope to have a life of excellence, satisfaction, and awe. Got it. Send me the T-shirt with the logo on it. Some of the messaging from the Hustle and Grind Culture has some truth to it. Happy things happen to people who do hard things.

Yet, to me, a glorious human experience must have some mess to it. Some times of "strategic laziness" in it. Some breathtaking days of serious sloppiness. Where we just allow ourselves to leave the bed unmade, the call unanswered, and the dishes unwashed. We're not machines, we're humans.

I guess what I'd like you to consider is to trust the flow more. Stop resisting your natural rhythms. Embrace the seasons when it doesn't seem like much is happening as the farmer accepts the fallow season as well as the times of harvest, understanding that without the first one the spectacular growth of the latter one would really not be possible. Honor the days where you have all the drive in the world. And rest more on the days that you don't.

5

Memorize The PENAM Principle

Have you ever wondered how you became the person that you are?

Ever considered what unfolded to make you *you*? (Which, by the way, is the only you exactly like you on the planet today.)

My answer can be said with a five-letter acronym: PENAM.

Yes, that's my answer.

Your core beliefs, basic behaviors, daily habits, and general ways of being were caused and created by the five forces that the acronym PENAM represents.

The "P" is for your *parents*. Sure, they most likely had good intentions, but the fact is that they also passed their faulty programming on to you. They did the best they could, based on what they knew and what *their* parents taught them. If they had money scars and had restricted thinking around financial abundance, you adopted those too (because a child assumes the thinking and subconsciously models the modes of behaving of the caregivers who teach them how the world works). If your parents believed that life was meant to be tragic, that most people are mean, and that human beings have no agency over the way things turn out, you accepted these beliefs and installed these habits. And rehearsed them so many times they actually became your truths and reality. Even if they were wrong.

The "E" stands for your *environment*. Your ecosystem has a dramatic impact on the way you show up each day. Allow mediocre inputs into your personal orbit, like violent TV shows, toxic news feeds and the messaging of narcissistic online influencers and, over time, these forces will degrade your positivity, performance, and joyfulness. Also, the surroundings you were raised in during the formative years that shaped your identity have had a huge effect on who you currently are in the world.

"N" stands for *nation*. If you grew up in a war zone or a country that suffers from social volatility, this will deeply affect the way you see things. If you are from a nation that is prosperous, stable and safe, this too creates a perceptual lens through which you process what's possible for you. And who you can become in the future.

"A" stands for your *associations*. Who you spend time with has an outsized impact on the way you think, feel, and act. Your friendship circle, for example, is a strong predictor of your income, lifestyle and lifetime impact. Enter relationships with drama queens and chaos kings and you will, over time, be profoundly shaped by these influences.

"M" stands for *media*. Each day, no matter where you live, you receive a constant torrent of hypnosis and seduction from many forms of media. These could include advertisements designed to make you buy products, suggestions on what life values are important, and subtle advice on how one should live in order to fit in with the crowd. All of this, over time, infects your self-identity and influences the way you interact with opportunity.

PENAM. These letters explain how you became you. Please

think about them. Discuss them with a pal. And meditate upon them alone. Because as you become more aware of the five forces that have shaped you, you grow in your self-mastery. And rise in the ability to make the better choices that are certain to generate more sensational results.

6
—

The Best Way to Start Is to Start

I'm on the road for a series of presentations to top leaders and heavyweight entrepreneurs as I write you this piece from my hotel room in Barcelona. I'm surrounded by the books I've brought on this trip (including *The Prophet* by Kahlil Gibran, *The Stories of My Life* by James Patterson, *The Bonfire of the Vanities* by Tom Wolfe, *The Great Crashes* by Linda Yueh, *Jellyfish Age Backwards* by Nicklas Brendborg, *The Art of Learning* by Josh Waitzkin, and *Why I Write* by George Orwell; yes, my suitcase is large), my morning journal and a pot of very good coffee. Yesterday I completed an intense day of media for *The Everyday Hero Manifesto*, which was recently released here. Tomorrow I'll be on a stage in service of six thousand people. I still get scared. Because after all these years, I still really, really, really care.

Earlier, one interviewer asked me a question I often hear after someone has heard a little of my ideology and methodology on leadership, exceptional performance, and making an honestly wealthy life you'll be proud of at the end: "So where do we begin?"

She added: "I also want to write a book and am wondering, where should I start?"

My answer was simple: "Just start."

It's really not that hard and there's no reason to complicate things as you materialize and optimize more of the genius you were born into. *The way you start is to start.* Often, overthinking and hypercomplicating how to get going is a sabotaging symptom of fear. In reality, you're resisting moving forward because you're frightened: of success, of failure, of being ridiculed, of standing out from your peer group.

How do you start a book? You write the first page. And tomorrow the second one. And the following day the third. Then, you keep on going until the darn thing is done. Yes, it's that simple (it's the execution on the commitment that's hard).

You absolutely must continue following through on the promises you set for yourself. To do anything less will destroy your self-respect and deny the world the magic you are here on Earth to make. Yes, advance at all costs! Through the self-doubt and the feelings the work is bad and all those shimmering attractions to digital diversions. Through the seducing desire for it to be easier (the finest things in life always come from the doing of uncomfortable things, right?).

How do you start the process of getting fit? You get up early tomorrow morning and do the first few push-ups. Then more the next day and even more after that. Until doing a ton of push-ups becomes easy. Because you've built yourself strong.

Yes, my friend. The way to start is to start. No excuses. Zero rationalizations. No postponements. Zero complaints. You just exercise your human will to take that first step. And then the next one. And on and on until you eventually become a master at getting the pursuits that are important to you done.

And as I wrote in *The Everyday Hero Manifesto*, "All change is hard at first, messy in the middle and gorgeous at the end."

So get going! Please. Your richest life is waiting. And nothing happens until you start.

7

Fears Are Ghost Stories

So you say you don't believe in ghosts.

Really? We all do.

... We say we can't be brave in scary situations, that we're not prepared enough or trained enough or good enough to accept a superb opportunity.

... We sell ourselves on the idea that we are unable to remain relentless when we feel like giving up.

... We tell ourselves that it's too hard to become the people we've always wanted to be.

... We argue for our weaknesses, obsess around our challenges and then practice our excuses to cover up our insecurities instead of living our greatness.

... We delude ourselves into thinking that those who are positive, creative, successful, and soulful are cut from a different cloth. And possess gifts that we don't have.

Most of our fears are big lies. Pure illusions. Blatant untruths. Ghost stories. If you get what I mean.

The pundit Osho told a story about a man who was climbing down from the summit of a soaring mountain. He'd been descending all day and the sun was setting. He carefully chose each step as the sky grew darker and dimmer. Suddenly, the climber lost his footing and, terrified that he'd fall thousands of feet into the abyss below, grabbed onto a branch.

All night, in staggering fear, the man hung from that branch thinking that if he let go, he'd plunge to his death. All night, he yelped for help. Yet no one heard his cries. He thought of all the things he hadn't yet done in his life, the potential he'd left unused, the growth he'd failed to experience, the human talents he never got to know, and the family he loved so much—all that he'd lose if he fell.

Then, at sunrise, the early light revealed a truth that startled the climber: just six inches below him was a wide ledge. In the darkness, he had failed to see it. He began to laugh, mildly at first and then uncontrollably. The man realized that his fear was only six inches deep. Below that, there was safety.

So change *your* narrative. Refuse to listen to the fairy tales that the ghost stories are selling you. They don't deserve to occupy your mind or limit your success, happiness, and serenity. They really are only six inches deep.

8

Stop Saying These Two Bad Words

. . . Tell someone to read the book that changed your life and they'll often reply with two words that amount to dirty swearing, in my mind.

. . . Recommend that your best friend watch the documentary that taught you how to build the skill that upgraded your artistry and maximized your productivity and they'll sometimes deploy the same bad words.

. . . Suggest to someone you care about that they heal a wound or remedy a flaw or turn their consuming problem into a satisfying solution and they'll all too often use the same refrain.

What are these two words that when used together amount to a symphony of negativity and seriously curb your commitment to personal growth—at least to my ears?

"I'll try."

Oh my. Oh my. Oh my.

. . . "I'll try" means you won't commit.

. . . "I'll try" means you're not really that invested.

... "I'll try" means you won't hold yourself accountable.

... "I'll try" means you aren't seriously that interested.

"I'll try" mostly means you're worried about making the necessary changes that need to be made to lead a life you love. And do remember that you cannot have the world you want without doing the things you must, if that makes sense.

"I'll try" is a reason bordering on an evasion offered by the majority to remove themselves from responsibility. This phrase dishonors your talents. And disrespects your genius.

"I'll try" is a violent robber of human potential, a thief of exceptional performance and a stone-cold killer of your biggest natural dreams.

"Do or do not. There is no try," advised Yoda of *Star Wars* fame. I do believe he was correct.

9

Be The Grown-Up in The Room

The other day, I had a profound conversation with someone who has been my friend for thirty years.

She shared that her father had recently passed away and her mother had died just before him, leading her brother to say, "I guess we're now the grown-ups in the room."

Hmmm. "The grown-ups in the room."

I don't know about you, but although I'm nearly sixty I pretty much feel the same as I did when I was a kid, at least in some ways. Strange, right?

On the outside, I look older and people guess I know more. And, of course, I have learned a ton and experienced so much life, so far.

Yet I still am trying to figure out many things. I still get confused by the unfolding of some events, ponder why some souls showed up on my path and wonder if life unfolds according to destiny, or if the whole ride is a random series of situations with no real meaning to them (which I doubt).

My friend's point was profound, for me. *Be the grown-up in the room.*

It reminded me that no one other than you will ultimately make your life better. No help is on the way and no savior in shining armor will magically show up to place a silver spoon inside your mouth (and a crown upon your head). No brigade of helpers or cavalry of rescuers is en route to make you into all you have ever wanted to become as a human being and mold your reality into something special, exciting, and fulfilling.

This makes me think of a young man I met when I visited a restaurant in Cape Town on one of my many trips to South Africa. He'd spent years in an extremely dangerous gang and then, one day, made the choice to break free. The owner of the restaurant wanted to help, so he gave him a job as a dishwasher. The young man used the chance to move up the ranks, falling in love with cooking in the process. Eventually, he became one of the top chefs at the place. Oh, and the establishment made it onto *The World's 50 Best Restaurants* list. And was named the best one in Africa.

I chatted with him at lunch. And asked what moved him to leave his old life. He paused thoughtfully, then replied: "I saw too many of my friends dead. I didn't want to die. So I had to change. I realized no one's going to do it for me, so I had to do it for myself."

Yes. You really do need to be the one to help you. And assume absolute personal responsibility for the way your life looks (and for making the improvements that will make it richer). Because in the room of life, you're the grown-up now.

10

Remember That Small Steps Make Giant Gains

For a few decades, I've been sharing a brain tattoo with my coaching clients and speaking audiences that I've been told has been enormously helpful to them, so I feel the need to share it with you: *Small, daily, seemingly insignificant improvements, when done consistently over time, lead to stunning results.*

A truly wealthy life happens more by evolution than by revolution. It's those constant and small microwins that, when done daily, evolve into a tsunami of victory. Which brings me to the Great Pyramid of Giza.

Recently, I was in Cairo. I had a day off and the event organizer generously arranged for a guided tour of this Seventh Wonder of the World. As we entered the marvelous monument that stands as testimony to human possibility, I learned that the Great Pyramid took twenty years to build. Two and a half million stones were needed, and nearly fifty thousand workers rallied to do the job. For over three thousand years, until the Eiffel Tower was created in 1887, this spellbinding structure stood as the highest one made by human hands.

The real formula that built the marvel? The monument was made by placing one block of stone upon another block of stone and another block upon that block, over and over and over. The focus wasn't on the pyramid but on the constant act of placing the blocks. The attention was on the process, not the goal. Please take a moment to reflect on this point.

We inhabit an age when so many of us want our dreams done instantly. Too many of us have forgotten the power of patience, the magic of steadiness, and the wonder of tiny triumphs made daily on the project that most inspires us—whether a health program or a love ambition, a financial objective, or a spiritual affair.

Your days are your life in miniature and as you craft each day, so you create your life. Consistency truly is the mother of mastery and the little things you do daily are so much more important than the big things that you might do annually.

I guess what I'm also suggesting is that you measure your success not by the achievement of the end result but instead by the depth of your commitment to the journey of making small steps in the direction of your brightest ideals (and by what staying on the path you've committed to makes of you as a person). Incrementally improving day by day is winning as far as I'm concerned. The completion of the project is just the icing on the cake. Not the real trophy.

Makes me reflect on the words of Scottish novelist Robert Louis Stevenson, who said: "Don't judge each day by the harvest you reap but by the seeds you plant."

Sometimes it doesn't look like your regular but minor acts of moving things forward are creating any progress. Yet—trust me—they are. Growth is often invisible, like seeds that are germinating underground that some time in the future will turn into towering trees. Just stay focused, dedicated, patient and aware that your tiny daily triumphs will eventually compound into remarkably big victories, over the passage of time.

Oh, and when those around you who don't get you (or are not really interested in supporting you) criticize or make fun of you, recall the words of prominent author Dale Carnegie: "Any fool can criticize, condemn and complain—and most fools do."

11

Worship Your Wounds

You're not broken, you're just human. You're not dysfunctional—you're just alive.

If you are willing to get into the game, exercise your native bravery, and take some risks to live your future vision, you're going to experience pain. The higher the mountain, the greater the danger.

It's not wrong for you to reach for the heavens (and seek to walk with the gods). No—it's ever so right. It means you're the hero of your life, that you have courage enough to take some chances and keep the faith in your mighty mission. What's the alternative? Dead person walking.

How wonderful that you still believe in you! And rare (in a culture of too many good people who have given up on their childhood hopes, accepted ordinary and are, unfortunately, passing through their best days as cyberzombies glued to white screens).

So you've been hurt. And yes, you've been scarred. I get you. I've been there too.

Yet may I humbly suggest that you celebrate your scars. And worship your wounds. Because they have served you beautifully.

Filling your life with unseen gifts, hidden treasures of wisdom, understanding, resilience, compassion, and greater intimacy with your specialness. Life unfolds for your fortune, never for your failure. Trust its strange ways. And keep going. Blessings you cannot yet fathom are coming. Your future is (so) bright.

12

The Human Who Reads The Most, Wins

BABLE: Book Accumulation Beyond Life Expectancy.

Yes. A not-guilty confession: this is my gorgeous affliction.

I do buy more books than I'll ever get to read. And my sense is you are the same.

You see, reading a book is having a conversation with the author. And the right conversation could set your life in a completely new direction. All it takes is one new idea to revolutionize your world, right?

And if one finds the right book, at the right time, the writer's stardust rubs off on you.

And the hand that eventually puts down the book is a fundamentally different hand.

While I was growing up, my father would say, "Cut back on buying things. Eat less food. Yet read more books."

A state leader who attended one of my leadership events in the Middle East once told me, "Robin, we eat three times a day to be fed. I read three times a day to become wise." I asked: "When do you read?" He replied: "When *don't* I read."

My home? Stacked with books.

... on creativity

... on productivity

... on history

... on psychology

... on business

... on economics

... on communication

... on vitality

... on longevity

... on character building

... on metaphysics

The piles of wisdom that surround me comfort me. They make me feel safe in a sometimes cruel yet mostly extraordinary world. They speak to me, of the promise of better days and the glories available to those who aspire.

I still seek that *one* book that completely shatters my limitations, resolves my inner conflicts, and lifts me to new heights of personal mastery and spiritual freedom. And although, given my age, I surely won't get through all the books I have purchased, I will bequeath (good word, right?) my library to my children. As my legacy.

Reading daily grows your knowledge base and allows you to transcend hard situations, make fewer mistakes, and predict the future. (Especially if you study history; Mark Twain said, "History doesn't repeat itself but it often rhymes.") In a world that wants you to think, do and be like the majority, reading voraciously makes you into someone who thinks for themselves. How much is that worth to you?

And each—and every—day while I get to be alive, I run The 45/15 Reading Rule: I read for (at least) forty-five minutes (but usually an hour) and then debrief what I've learned in my learning notebook for fifteen, so I understand the concept more deeply and *apply* it in my life. Ideation without execution becomes a delusion.

So, fellow bookworm ...

... In a world consumed by digital invasion and addictive trivial diversion, re-spark your highest love affair with books. (Written are best, yet audiobooks also work wonderfully.) And spend fine time—each day—within the pages and ideas of legendary thinkers who will remind you of what is possible. And rekindle your connection with your hidden curiosity.

Because the human who reads the most, wins.

13

Deep Growth Is Meant to Feel Weird

All change is hard at first, messy in the middle and gorgeous at the end. All change is hard at first, messy in the middle and gorgeous at the end. All change is hard at first, messy in the middle and gorgeous at the end. Okay—I'll stop repeating this if you promise you'll never forget it.

Intense personal change and outright human transformation are meant to be scary and difficult and confusing at first. Otherwise, it wouldn't be real change. And there would be no value in it.

Did you know that the space shuttle used more fuel in the first sixty seconds after liftoff than it would consume during its entire voyage around the circumference of the Earth?

This is because at the beginning, it had to overcome the terrifically strong forces of gravity that wanted to keep it on the ground. So it took a ton of energy and a large degree of work to push the vehicle higher and higher—at that early stage—until "escape velocity" was reached. The forces of gravity had then been transcended. The spacecraft was free. To soar.

When it comes to you making the changes that you must make to lead the life you most desire, you're sort of like that space shuttle.

You need to exert a ton of energy and do hard work to overcome your previous ways of operating. To leave behind *your* gravitational forces (the ones that have restricted your original greatness).

So it's *super* hard at first. That doesn't mean there's anything wrong. It just means the change you're making is worthwhile, valuable, and rich. Everything you now find easy you once found hard, yes?

The new habits, skills and behaviors will get easier to implement as the days go by—be sure of this. Things always get easier with practice. And because you couldn't do something yesterday doesn't mean you can't get it done today. You're one day better. And twenty-four hours stronger.

14
—

Expect The Best from People (and You'll Mostly Get It)

I'm mildly embarrassed to share this story, yet I must be honest with you. So here goes.

Recently, while on the road, I was in a rustic restaurant that I don't visit often yet always love when I do.

It's in a small Swiss town and does exquisite "geschnetzeltes Kalbfleisch an Rahmsauce mit Cognac verfeinert mit Rösti," which simply means veal in a cream sauce with cognac and shredded potatoes. (I'm just trying to impress you with my nonexistent Swiss German fluency.)

I was with a good friend and we enjoyed a delicious lunch together, talking about films, family, and the future. It was precious. In a straightforward sort of way.

At the end, when the bill arrived, and knowing that I had a reservation at the same restaurant for the next day, I asked the owner if it would be possible for me to have a quiet table off to the side when I returned. I wanted to work on the manuscript of this book in a soulful space that enriched my inspiration.

She was polite yet slightly curt and explained it would be

impossible because "We are full tomorrow and it will be very hard to put you at a table in this room."

I thought that was a little odd.

Sure, I understood they were full, yet I did have a reservation (made many weeks earlier) and didn't really understand why she couldn't find a single space that was quiet and maybe even in a corner, as the room we were in had many corners.

And I must admit that for a little while after my friend and I left the restaurant, I felt bad, ruminating over the rejection and concocting stories about her coldness, mild arrogance, and implicit meanness. Sorry. But as your mentor from afar, I do need to tell you that that's just what I did.

So the next morning, I woke up early, worked out in the gym on the elliptical machine, had my coffee, wrote in my journal, and reread parts of this book. I then made my way to this special restaurant to enjoy another lunch. This time, alone.

As I approached the restaurant, I saw a man standing outside in what appeared to be a leather skirt, a thick fur jacket and the kind of colorful attire a Viking would wear. Hmmm. Interesting. (You know I can't make this sort of thing up.)

As I walked in, I saw that the entire main room was full of fellow Vikings—or whatever these good people were dressing up to be. They were laughing loudly, clapping passionately, stomping their feet thunderously, and bellowing speeches at the top of their hoarse voices. I guessed it was some kind of guild meeting or important event to honor the traditional life of the region.

The main room was not only packed with the hell-raisers, but they were also enthusiastically drinking unusually large amounts of darkly colored beer.

Thank God I wasn't in that room! I would have been the only non-Viking in the place and the noisiness would have given me a headache, destroying any chance of me writing anything good over the solo lunch while attempting to enjoy my excellent meal.

It gets better.

The same woman who had rejected me yesterday politely escorted me past the rowdy Vikings and their furry fur coats and dark-colored ale into a very quiet and actually quite romantic little room that I'd never been in. There were flowers on the tables and candles carefully placed over white linen. Angels in white capes played harps while doodle puppies danced. (Okay, that last line isn't true. But the room really was utterly *fantastic*.)

It gets even better. The owner of the restaurant then put me into a lovely corner seat. With no one next to me and few people around me. She smiled a huge smile. And warmly welcomed me back. "Have a wonderful lunch, you handsome devil," she said softly. (Okay, the "handsome devil" part isn't true, but the rest absolutely is.)

So my perception of being rejected was a hallucination. The truth was that she was trying to protect me from the boisterous Vikings.

The lesson for us? Not everything is about us. Stop taking everything personally. Most people are incredibly good and profoundly decent. The more we expect the best from others, the more encouragement they'll receive to show it to us.

The German literary icon Johann Wolfgang von Goethe said it far more eloquently than I could in a million years: "If we treat people as if they were what they ought to be, we help them become what they are capable of becoming."

And as you do this regularly, you not only help other people to grow, you grow too. Which makes you a really wealthy person. Very rich, indeed.

15
—

Eat Alone Fairly Often

How do you grow braver? Easy. You regularly do frightening things. The discomfort of growth is always smaller than the heartbreak of regret. And at the last hour of your final day, it won't be all the things you did that will bring you sorrow but all the things you didn't do. All the dreams you didn't pursue and all the fears you didn't face and all the opportunities you didn't seize and all the travels you didn't take and all the books you didn't read and all the love you didn't give. (Kindly read this last line twice because it's really important for you.)

A great way to start optimizing your self-confidence and overall fearlessness is to eat alone. Today, I'm eating alone in a simple Italian restaurant, in the village near the farmhouse as I write this mentoring message to you.

In my experience, most people would rather eat at home if they are alone than go to a restaurant and sit alone at a table in a public place, surrounded by others having the time of their lives.

Or, if we do go out alone, we pull out our phones, scroll through our feeds and watch videos of quirky people doing bizarre dance moves. Or celebrities leaving Hollywood restaurants in colorful outfits (or causing public scenes) as flashes go off. Or influencers hawking the latest beauty product while wearing a face mask.

But to just sit there alone is actually a rare thing. Without a device. With zero escape routes. In a crowded restaurant. With others nearby laughing and drinking and eating and merrily connecting.

To risk being judged as not good enough to be with another human over a meal. To dare to be considered an oddball and weird and eccentric by having the audacity to eat alone. To be willing to be stared at by people who avert their eyes when you catch them looking at you. Well, that's the stuff magic-workers are made of. And yes, my friend, that means you.

The way you do one thing creates the way you do everything. To be brave in one area is practice for being brave in every area. And being your bravest self is so key to leading your richest life. *Real* rich. Not fake rich. As Frank Herbert, the author of *Dune*, wrote:

> I must not fear. Fear is the mind killer. Fear is the little death that brings total obliteration. I will face my fear. I will permit it to pass over me and through me. And when it has gone past I will turn the inner eye to see its path. Where fear has gone there will be nothing. Only I will remain.

16

It's Wise to Keep a Journal

On most mornings of the past twenty-five years of my life I've run a morning ritual that has been ever so valuable to my personal growth, increasing creativity, professional learning, and spiritual ascension: writing in a journal.

In *The Everyday Hero Manifesto*, I shared the story of how ten years' worth of my private journals vanished—yet that's another story. Maybe I'll share it fully with you if we meet in person sometime in the future.

To put it simply, there are six primary reasons why you should embrace the daily routine of journaling:

1. Journaling promotes wise behavior.

Vague thinking creates vague results. Writing in a notebook about your desires, intentions and commitments increases your clarity, and clarity is the DNA of mastery. To ask yourself good questions—such as, "What must happen over the coming hours for this to be a day of my life lived well?" or "What three small wins will I accomplish today to make things better than yesterday?"—raises your focus and dramatically improves your willpower to get your goals done. By carefully reflecting on what you wish to create, your performance becomes more concentrated and successful. Journaling promotes promise keeping.

2. Journaling increases artistry and captures peak ideas.

A genius-grade idea not noted will rarely be remembered. Writing down your insights not only deepens your understanding but often stimulates further ones. Keeping a notebook is also a superb discipline to help you find excellent solutions to weighty problems you've been working on and to record life lessons you're learning.

3. Journaling encourages you to record your magical moments so you get to live them twice.

A beautiful meal or a magnificent sunset or an oceanside walk with one you love, when written about, not only embeds the experience in your mind, body, heart, and soul—it gives you the chance to live it again. Imagine the rises in your energy, gratitude, happiness and momentum when you're regularly re-experiencing your best moments. And training your brain on where you are winning rather than upon the frustrations you may be facing.

The pre-eminent positive psychologist Sonja Lyubomirsky has found through her research that the happiest people are not the ones with the easiest circumstances (only 10 percent of one's happiness is due to external reality, she has discovered) but the ones with the largest gratefulness. And their appreciation is not random and disordered but "deliberate gratitude." Your journal is an excellent place to list the blessings in your life deliberately and regularly so that the negativity bias of the human brain gets rewired for unbeatable positivity.

4. Journaling is prayer on paper.

Prayer is a powerful force multiplier in the manifestation of your ideals. Every prayer is heard by your higher power and every thanksgiving makes you stronger, wiser, and more tranquil. So write down what you seek and record what you want to see more of in your world. What you focus on really does grow and what you think about expands.

5. Journaling gives you a monastery to process through pain, sorrow, and other challenging emotions.

During the icy winters of my life—when things felt very severe and quite disappointing—pouring my suffering onto a crisp, blank page was enormously healing. Science confirms the same. Pain suppressed always comes back to haunt you in unexpected ways. Writing about your hurts in a journal allows you a safe space to process through them to a release. Because to heal a wound you need to feel the wound. And to let go of a cut you need to do the inner work to clear it.

6. Journaling allows you the gorgeous opportunity to record your colorful life.

Henry Wadsworth Longfellow wrote: "A life that is worth writing at all, is worth writing minutely and truthfully." Wise words, right? Your life matters and is utterly unique and a thing of immeasurable beauty (in all its highs and lows). So isn't it worth recording?

17

Your Hurters Are Your Helpers

I'm writing this piece for you in my spartan writing room at the farmhouse. The window is open, early spring air fills the space, and I hear a couple of sheepdogs barking in the distance. A rooster crows far too loudly for my serenity. The olive trees look enchanting and the early morning sunshine illuminates the vineyards off into the distance as I sip a simple cup of espresso (one of the tiny wonders that I adore waking up for).

Okay. Let's talk about your hurters. Those people who played you, misused you, and betrayed you. The ones who broke your trust, stole your kindness, and perhaps even left you a little cynical, critical, and closed.

They showed up in your life for a reason, I do believe.

You see, the people who cause you pain can actually be the same ones who introduce you to your power. And the suffering they have caused can—*if you choose*—become a gateway into strengths you didn't know you had, before the harm was done.

Neale Donald Walsch of *Conversations with God* fame wrote a short children's book that has helped me immeasurably. It's called *The Little Soul and the Sun.*

Short story short, it's about two souls who meet each other. Before becoming human beings.

This might seem far out and if it's weird to you, I totally get it. Yet it seems pretty possible to me. Just because we don't believe in something—or understand a novel concept that bends our reality—doesn't mean it's untrue, right?

Anyway. The two souls have a conversation about a promise. The little soul said to the friendly soul that it wanted to know the fullest extent of all its specialness, powerfulness, and wisdom (just like you). And so, the second soul said it would help by doing something bad to the little soul in its lifetime. The friendly soul was asked why it would agree to reduce itself from its natural glory so it could do something hurtful, and it replied, "Because I love you."

And so, both souls became human beings. And sure enough, the friendly soul who wanted the little soul to experience its greatness by learning how to love (when it was toughest to love) and to forgive (when it was hardest to forgive) and to be noble (when being decent was demanding) caused deep difficulty to the little soul.

And the little soul did exercise its specialness, learning to forgive the other soul for its mean act. Because it knew that that soul did so out of love. To help the little soul remember all it truly was.

I share this wonderful parable with you because maybe—just maybe—it reflects reality. What if your past isn't a prison to stay locked in but a school meant to be learned from? What if every single person who has somehow hurt you—by lying to you or betraying you or attacking you or being mean to you—has done this to somehow help you?

To push you out of a life of constant comfort and low personal growth into a *far* richer one where you, by standing in the fires of hardship, discover the great virtues of the best human beings. Virtues such as wisdom, tolerance, patience, resilience, persistence, forgiveness, and lovingness. To aid you in becoming the creator, warrior, leader, hero, and truly wealthy human that your destiny only wishes you would be.

18

Hang with Clowns, Expect a Circus

I'd like us to revisit the point I made in an earlier mentoring session because I want to reinforce it for you. The one about being thoughtful and careful about who you spend time with. Because you can handcraft an exceptionally great life or stay with toxic people, but you can't do both.

You become your associations, and your conversations noticeably affect the way you see the world as well as how you show up within it. If you spend your days with victims, disbelievers, and criticizers, their thought viruses and emotional shadows will degrade your brilliance.

Investing your valuable hours (once spent, they are lost forever) with those who deflate your joy, mock your ambitions, and pollute you with their poison is a sure way to stay stuck, betraying your promise to realize meaningful things, experience genuine beauty, and live with high levels of freedom.

So may I please encourage you to do a courageous audit of the people you've allowed into your circle and remove (or spend far less time with) the negative ones, while increasing your bonds with those who fuel your faith in opportunity, bravery, and human possibility.

Because if you hang with clowns, you'd better expect a circus.

19

Don't Let Self-Care Ruin Your Self-Worth

What I feel the need to share with you now is the importance of not confusing the essential practice of self-care—which is all about protecting your purest mind, healing your good heart, fortifying a healthy body, and nourishing your sovereign spirit, among other things—with the heroic goal of living daringly and pursuing a creative mission that will increase your self-worth.

Many people use "inner work" as a way to avoid facing fears and doing the outer work that will make their genius real. Look, I've been an evangelist for growing a rich interior life for over a quarter of a century. When I first began as an author and speaker, people laughed at me when I spoke of the power of a great morning routine, daily meditation as a means to stay strong and calm, walking in nature to raise positivity and improve creativity, resting more to extend lifespan and building one's life around a cause. Self-care is the foundation of a cheerful, balanced, healthy, and peaceful life.

Yet sincerely successful people—and this is an important point—never use the wise need for self-care as an excuse from doing the sometimes hard things that also make a human life excellent.

They don't spend all of their finest days in a bathtub perfumed with bath salts, while fresh camomile tea brews and mystical meditation music plays, as someone gives them a foot massage.

To be great, you absolutely need to be focused, productive, relentless, and undefeatable in passionately pursuing projects that—though difficult at times—push you to reveal your highest (and most gifted) self. The consistent achieving of seemingly impossible things introduces you to strengths, talents, and powers you didn't even know you had. And translating your deeply inspired dreams into disciplined daily results leaves a trail of victory that electrifies your self-worth. You'll love yourself more when you do more of the things that you don't love doing (but are important to do). And, trust me, you'll be happier by becoming even more productive.

So do both. Make good self-care a top priority. An exceptional life is a direct reflection of inner wellbeing. Yet balance this with the ongoing building of a base of supreme self-worth, born of elite performance, extraordinary achievement, and the consistent making of outright masterpieces.

20

Become a Yes Person

The other day—before I walked on stage to deliver a leadership keynote to nine thousand business leaders in London—I had a great chat with the son of a renowned speaker.

He told me that although his father is elderly, he still says yes to everything. *Everything.*

Yes to speaking events and yes to writing more books and yes to coaching young entrepreneurs. Yes to traveling to many different continents and yes to reading new books and yes to fresh challenges and yes to new friendships and yes to trying exciting adventures.

I guess that makes him a YES man.

And that's pretty fantastic to me. Our tiny planet, going through such tumult, needs more of his kind. People with the wisdom to put down their devices and inhabit the wonders of the present moment. Individuals who really do understand that the illusion of safety is always more dangerous than the discomfort of growth. Human beings who refuse to live the same year eighty times and call it a life.

Fear and doubt and disbelief and apathy and mediocrity and cynicism and entitlement keep us small, blocking our native access to excellence, productivity, happiness, and the leadership that is our birthright.

So—just maybe—the most powerful word in the world is one of the simplest: "YES."

To increase the first form of wealth, I enthusiastically encourage you to say yes to the risky new project that will push your growth. Say yes to the trip you've been postponing for years. Say yes to giving the speech that spooks the daylights out of you and the new relationship that stretches you emotionally and the book that seems so hard to read you don't want to read it yet you know you must, as it carries the wisdom your strongest self most wishes you would know.

Your greatness and your magic depend on this. And your personal honor demands it of you. To say yes, far more often.

THE 2ND FORM OF WEALTH

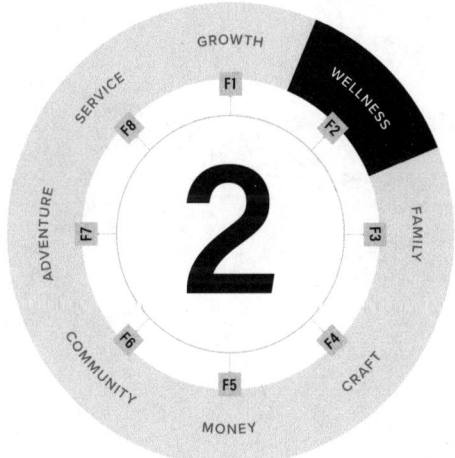

Wellness

The Steadily Optimize Your Health Habit

Good health is not valued until sickness comes.
—Thomas Fuller, English historian

The 2nd Form of Wealth
Wellness | Quick Overview

Health is a type of wealth. If you don't feel good physically, mentally, emotionally, and spiritually, all the money, possessions and fame in the world mean nothing. Lose your wellness (which I pray you never will) and I promise you that you'll spend the rest of your days trying to get it back.

In one wisdom tradition, it is spoken: "When we are young, we are willing to sacrifice all of our health for the pursuit of wealth and once we are old, we become willing to sacrifice all of our wealth for even one day of good health."

I had a conversation with a great and true friend yesterday. His uncle was a billionaire who recently passed away. Softly, my pal spoke about his uncle's serious illness, and how, near the end, he often told his family that he would have given away his entire fortune to get his once-taken-for-granted wellness back.

There is no point hustling and grinding, overworking and not sleeping to reach your personal Mount Everest, only to end up sick in a sterile hospital room. With tubes down your throat, with needles in your veins, and bound to a bed. I know you know what I mean.

And when I write of protecting your top health, I must emphasize that I'm not only referring to your physical realm. To lead your richest life you also need to nourish the health of your mind, guard the wellness of your emotional universe, and regularly and carefully feed your spiritual life. So you consistently feel happy, and profoundly peaceful. For how can one say they are wealthy without a life of positivity, wonder, and soulfulness?

21

Take a Bath in a Forest

Okay, maybe not literally (although if you want to that's fine by me). A highly popular practice in Japan is *shinrin-yoku*, which means "forest bath." Scientific research has confirmed that walking in the woods significantly reduces your blood pressure and any fatigue, anxiety, depression, and cognitive confusion.

Doing a hike in nature also lowers the stress hormone cortisol and improves your happiness levels. This routine is not only excellent for your mental, physical, and emotional health, it's terrific for your spiritual vigor. By being close to the earth, grounding among the trees, breathing in fresh air, and getting away from our noisy world, you'll reconnect with the highest part of you. The one that knows the answers to your deepest questions, has the wisdom to lead you to your best decisions, and is connected to all of life itself.

Walking in nature is also one of my favorite practices to stimulate creativity. The celebrated English writer Virginia Woolf would take daily walks. Charles Darwin, the legendary scientist, took three forty-five-minute walks each day for most of his life. Vincent van Gogh said, "Try to walk as much as you can and keep your love of nature."

I recommend that before you start your workday, you take a

fifteen-minute walk near trees, plants, and flowers. This protocol will change the game in terms of your ability to concentrate, the extent of your energy, and your overall productivity.

As human beings, we are built to be in nature. And this communion will not only optimize your wellness, it'll bring far more awe, fascination, and beauty into your life. And wouldn't that be a healthy thing?

22

Know Your Genes Are Not Your Destiny

I'm truly fascinated by the field of epigenetics. "Epi" means "above" in Greek. So epigenetics is simply the study of the factors above and beyond your genetic code that regulate the turning on and turning off of the genes you were born with, if that makes sense.

In the past, the common understanding was that the genes you inherited from your parents determined your physical destiny. The "nature versus nurture" debate has been solved and scientific research now confirms that the way human beings develop in terms of our physical and mental health involves *both* the natural genes we have received from previous generations and environmental factors such as the quality of our thinking, our daily fitness habits, our eating behaviors, and our sleep protocols.

Yes, your environment and lifestyle choices have a powerful ability to alter the expression of the genes you have inherited. *You need not be a victim to your genetics.* By installing healthier practices such as early morning exercise, managing stress through regular meditation, or taking the walks in nature (as I mentioned in the last chapter), breathing properly, eating chemical-free and unprocessed food, fasting intermittently, consuming less alcohol, taking at least a day a week away from digital devices, exposing ourselves to cold showers or hot baths, and resting deeply, we can actually turn off genes within our genomes that would have caused us to function poorly or get sick and turn on the ones that will optimize our wellness and lead to a long, disease-free life.

So as your caring mentor from afar I suggest that you never give away your power to become the healthiest person you know to excuses around the genetics that earlier generations have passed on to you. And start (or increase) your dedication to constantly executing the habits that I hope will make you live forever.

23

The Shortest Chapter in The History of Health Inspiration?

Few habits will help you as much as moving your body vigorously daily. It's the elixir for an exceptional life. So as a champion of you becoming your absolute best I must passionately say: If you're not exercising now, get up and get going!

And if you're already exercising consistently then turn up your enthusiasm. And stretch your physical game. *Today*.

Life's just too short not to get really fit. And as Mark Twain said, "Continuous improvement is better than delayed perfection."

24

See Food as Medicine

"Let food be thy medicine and medicine be thy food," instructed the Father of Medicine, Hippocrates.

Your diet profoundly influences your general wellbeing. Blueberries, apples, salmon, and green tea have been proven to promote your happiness, for example. Foods such as avocados, Brazil nuts, and eggs have been scientifically shown to be strong fatigue-fighters and to deliver the energy for you to be at your best.

In a paper published in *The Lancet*, it was reported that poor nutrition was responsible for eleven million deaths globally, within the twelve-month period of the study. A diet high in sodium was the leading risk factor for this mortality. So my gentle yet strong encouragement is that, today, you eat more cleanly, clearly and intentionally. "If it doesn't hang from a tree, grow in the ground, or have a mother, don't eat it" is a good adage to follow (unless you're a vegan). And do remember that you'll never feel good eating bad food.

As strange as it sounds, I also consider water as medicine. As a rule, you should drink four to six glasses of water each day, which will reward you beautifully with numerous health benefits, such as increased blood circulation, enhanced skin vitality and brain functioning, decreased joint pain, a healthier heart, and enriched mitochondrial function, which ensures slower aging and greater longevity.

I don't wish to get into the topic of which diets work best because I don't really like diets (creating a sustainable *lifestyle* that includes eating wholesome food is one thousand times smarter), and one size doesn't fit all.

Having said this, I need to tell you that one of the best investments I've ever made was having my genome analyzed (a quick online search will give you the test providers) because it showed precisely what foods work best for me, given which of my genes were optimal and which ones could be enhanced via the food I eat. I'll simply encourage you to see food as a category of medicine and to eat what's best for you. Your mindset, moods, energy, vitality, and vigor will thank you. Forever.

25

Defend The Health of Your Mind

Gratefulness really is the antidote to worry. And helpfulness is most certainly a splendid cure for fear. Please allow me to explain.

First, no section on health could be complete without talking about mental fitness (what's the point of a healthy body with an unwell mind, right?). Protecting your mental condition also elevates your physical life. So let's drop into a few of my recommendations to keep your psychology at its absolute peak.

Human beings have a built-in negativity bias. You and I are automatically hardwired to survey our surroundings and actively focus on the threats. This cognitive tendency served us well thousands of years ago when we faced relentless danger in our environments. This evolutionary instinct allowed our ancestors to survive. But now the saber-toothed tigers are gone, the chance of straying from the herd and starving is far less, and the risk of being killed by a member of an unfriendly tribe is generally nearly zero.

Yet we still suffer from the brain's drive to look for problems, stay stuck on disappointments, and give a whole lot more importance to the situations in our days that are negative versus positive.

... We ruminate on an unpleasant comment made to us (and sometimes remember it for years) and forget about all the praise that we have been blessed to receive.

... We concentrate on the irritating traits of a coworker rather than upon their friendly qualities.

... We constantly re-live traumatic experiences instead of letting them go, moving on, and enjoying the gifts of the moment.

... We are twice as likely to avoid doing something that could enrich our lives massively (due to the fear of losing what we have) than to experience the pleasure of gaining the rewards that the new behavior will bring (read this twice, please).

To rewire your negativity bias into a more positive focus, for far greater happiness and mental wellness, I offer you four regular practices:

Positivity Practice #1: Write a "How Could This Be Worse Paragraph." In your journal, record a few lines describing how the scenario that is bothering you could be *dramatically* worse. This will shift your thinking from a state of toxicity to one of thankfulness, providing you with a sense of perspective over your problems.

Positivity Practice #2: Get Good at Savoring. So many of us are rushing through our lives like we're running from a five-alarm fire. We fill our calendars to overflowing, obsess with maximizing productivity within every waking hour and neglect what we know are the essentials of a fully lived life to chat online with people we don't even like. Positive psychologists have found that the happiest, healthiest people have a common trait: they make a point of "savoring." This means that when something good happens they slow down and take it in. Actively and consistently make the time to mindfully appreciate and reflect on your blessings, even if these are as simple as a good cup of coffee in the morning, a roof over your head, or a child who loves laughing.

Positivity Practice #3: Improve Your Self-Talk. Most of us would never speak as harshly to others as we speak to ourselves. Start being kinder to yourself—giving yourself more praise for good deeds, validation for being true to yourself, and celebration for all you are becoming. You've overcome so many challenges, accomplished so many good things, and been a source of encouragement for so many people. Talk to yourself in a way that reflects this progress.

Positivity Practice #4: Be Actively Helpful. To give of yourself in service of others is to release yourself from worry, negativity, and anxiety. Actively and consistently ask yourself, "How may I make the lives of others better?" and then go ahead and take the action. "The best way to find yourself is to lose yourself in the service of others," advised Mahatma Gandhi.

The more you practice these four central positivity practices, the more you'll restructure your neural pathways and beat the negativity bias that blocks you from your joy, vitality, and serenity.

26

Microdose Meditation

I'm at a small cottage on a South African vineyard as I write you this mentoring message. I've come here for inspiration and seclusion so I can finish this part of the book. Country music plays, the sun rises above the mountains in the distance and I am amused by the honest laughter of the workers walking among the ancient vines.

Let us begin this chapter with a question: What's the point of having everything society has told you that you should strive to own if, once you have it, you feel completely empty? And are constantly concerned about losing everything you have?

I've discovered that the key to a great life is to be in the world yet not be attached to it. Do your best, then let life do the rest, right? And everything that happens happens for a marvelously good reason—even if in the moment things look bad, yes? Human existence is all a game, of sorts. Participate in the game because we do live on planet Earth so that's sort of what we've signed up for. Yet don't forget that it's all an illusion in so many ways and that what the majority tells you is important is generally very unimportant.

I guess what I'm suggesting is please don't spend the best days of your life climbing a mountain only to realize when it's too late that you've climbed the wrong one. Wasting a life is a tragic mistake.

Which brings me to meditation. You don't need to do it every day, although I really think you should do it every day, even if you're a business titan, a financial trader, a top athlete, or a state leader. Actually, if you pursue any of these occupations you *must* meditate. Reminds me of another of Mahatma Gandhi's statements: "I have so much to accomplish today that I must meditate for two hours instead of one."

And even if you're not in a high-pressure role, I still strongly and lovingly urge you to create a regular meditation practice. It'll keep you centered and strong amid challenges, thinking optimistically, and feeling profoundly relaxed. So you make your clearest decisions and perform at your best.

Meditation will also reduce the inflammation that causes disease and will help you live a whole lot longer. And you don't even have to do it for a long time each session.

I adore one-hour or two-hour meditation periods, yet you can microdose it, if you like. If you can't do sixty minutes, do thirty. And if you can't do thirty, do ten. And if you can't do ten, just do five.

Something is better than nothing. And *every session counts*. It really, really does. Making progress always works better than seeking perfection. Steady gains all work together to get you closer to a life of constant contentment and lasting inner freedom.

27

Practice The Naked Sunbathing Rule

Okay, maybe you don't need to be naked (unless you like to be, and that's fine with me).

The point I'm encouraging you to consider today, as you work on building the second form of wealth, is the dazzling value of spending time in the sunshine (not too much because that's bad but a reasonable amount of time because that's good). Each and every day. Or whenever it's sunny.

Moderate (ten to twenty minutes) sun exposure increases your serotonin levels, which increases your happiness levels. This amount of sunbathing has also been reported to raise vitamin D measures by 5,000 IU. Some research even suggests that a short period in the sun between 8 AM and noon helps with weight loss. Oh, and morning sunbathing—again, in moderation—allows sunlight into your eyes, which increases your mental focus, overall daytime alertness and the depth of your sleep.

And get this: the *Journal of Internal Medicine* reported a study involving thirty thousand Swedes that found that those who spent a small time in the sun daily lived between six months to two years longer than those who did not.

Now, of course, too much exposure to the UV rays of sunshine is carcinogenic. You know that.

Yet a little more time sunbathing just might be the habit that grows your positivity, enriches your tranquility, and extends your richest life.

28

A Sweaty Workout
Is Never a Silly Idea

I woke up this morning and did not feel like working out. My mind came up with a litany of excellent excuses: "A rest day would be good today" (I didn't need a rest day because I had one a few days earlier) and "I'm an artist so why not enjoy the moment?" And "I'll work twice as hard in the gym tomorrow."

Yet I reached into the vast reservoir of willpower that we all have within us (it's like a muscle that grows stronger with use) and pushed myself to go to the gym. Excuses are liars and procrastination is a thief. And I remembered what boxing legend Muhammad Ali taught me when he said: "I hated every minute of training but I said, 'Don't quit. Suffer now and live the rest of your life as a champion.'"

And guess what? The workout got easier the more I got moving. Yes. I turned up the music (it was "Anthem" by Greta van Fleet) and picked up the pace (I was running). The more I sweated the happier I felt. The longer I ran the more energy I had. Once I was done, I felt *absolutely fantastic*. The decision to do what I was resisting completely changed the texture, vibe and energy of my entire day.

My lesson for you here, my friend? Easy. Though you may wake up thinking that exercising today is a bad idea, by the time you do it, I'd be willing to bet my trusted and muddy mountain bike that you realize it was a very good one. Because you'll always feel so much better after a spirited workout than you did before you started it.

29

Do a 30-Day Zero-Sugar Challenge

When I mentor a billionaire or advise a start-up entrepreneur or counsel a famous actor, I'll often put them on a series of thirty-day challenges. This practice works extremely well.

   . . . If the goal is to get fit, it might be thirty days of walking ten thousand steps each morning.

   . . . If the focus is greater positivity and more mental toughness, this may mean thirty full days of going without any complaining.

   . . . If the objective is a far higher quality of work, the challenge could involve thirty days of going dark from social media or traveling to a seaside retreat to get their magnum opus done.

You get my drift. And the concept really does work incredibly well (especially if you keep a daily log or use an online habit tracker). If you miss a day that's okay, don't beat yourself up. Get back on the horse tomorrow. Which oddly brings me to sugar.

It's completely poison, you know? It can lead to a leaky gut, diabetes, fatty liver disease, and heart problems. It can promote cancer, create brain disturbances, and increase metabolic disorders. Get it out of your life and your physical wellness, mental focus, energy levels, and longevity will soar.

Yes, for thirty days avoid sugar. The first few days will be a struggle as your sugar tooth screams for ice cream or candy or chocolate or sodas, but then your body will adapt, your cravings will be for more natural food, and you'll start feeling really, really, really great. Remember that all change is hard at first, messy in the middle, and gorgeous at the end. And that nothing tastes as good as top health feels.

30

Commit to a Dopamine Detox

One of the best moves you'll ever make to get the wealth of your wellness to a whole new level is to free yourself of the all-too-common relentless craving for dopamine.

The very design of social media apps is built around raising the release of this neuroregulator, which makes you feel driven and delighted. Each time you see likes on a post you've created, your brain's reward center is activated, which then causes the release of more dopamine.

Likewise, watching television shows full of action, keeping a hectic schedule, eating sweet treats and engaging in other escapes such as over-texting, endless online scrolling, compulsive clothes buying, and consuming alcohol breed a dopamine feedback loop. Doing these things gives you instant sensations of pleasure, which in turn releases dopamine in your brain, which in turn motivates more of this pleasure-seeking (yet often toxic) behavior.

Here's the key piece of information to know: as you produce more dopamine, you begin to need more dopamine for the same high. This leads not only to a dopamine deficit but also to the psychological phenomenon of hedonic adaptation where you do all the things that once made you happy, yet you now feel apathy. You begin to feel jaded and notice that few things in life give you feelings of joy anymore, which pushes you to pursue even more stimulation with the hope of feeling more alive. What a mess!

The solution? Do a "dopamine detox." Yours could be five or even ten days long and include:

- ... no device checking during the first two hours after you wake up
- ... full social media fasting
- ... avoidance of TV, video games, and even music for the detox period
- ... eating simple, lighter foods at home instead of heavy foods in a restaurant
- ... being in solitude, silence, and stillness for a few hours each day
- ... no alcohol or other addictive mood enhancers during the time of the program

Doing this will recalibrate your dopamine production, prevent the hijack of your brain's reward system, and allow you to break bad habits such as endlessly watching social media feeds or seeking silly videos, and filling every waking hour with "hustling and grinding" just so you have even a little bit more of feeling good.

I guess what I'm also suggesting is that you slow your life down and simplify your days. Do less to live more. This makes me think of what Henry David Thoreau wrote in his wonderful book *Walden*:

> I went to the woods because I wished to live deliberately, to front only the essential facts of life, and see if I could not learn what it had to teach, and not, when I came to die, discover that I had not lived.

31

Become a Professional Sleeper

To feel more wonderful and become a whole lot healthier, sleep much more. Last night, I slept ten hours! This isn't my normal routine, yet oh me oh my do I feel fantastic today!

Tons of reputable science is telling you, me, and the rest of the good souls walking the planet today that sleep deprivation is the number one way to cut your lifespan short.

Although I've been encouraging people to rise before dawn for ages (many millions of people have read *The 5AM Club*, installed *The 20/20/20 Formula* for a world-class morning routine, and dramatically upgraded their lives by it), I haven't said that this should be done at the expense of rest. Not at all.

Sleep is not a luxury but a necessity. (Could you please read that line five more times and then tattoo it onto your brain and etch it deeply into your heart?) Because good rest lies at the bedrock of a gorgeous life.

Research confirms that when we sleep, a mechanism is invoked that washes the brain. Proper sleep rinses the brain of toxins, repairs brain cells damaged by stress, and allows for memories to be assembled then integrated in the most efficient way possible.

Good rest also grows your creativity, advances your productivity (via refueling your energy), and even ensures you're emotionally steady (by managing the amygdala—the part of the brain that releases stress hormones in response to a threat—and reducing limbic hijack). Ever notice how easy it is to overreact and make the bad choices that cause big problems when you've had a night of poor sleep? I'd almost go out on a limb and say the majority of our mistakes are made when we are tired. A splendid night of sleep restores perspective and just makes *everything* better.

I invite you to build a smart sleep habit stack, so you can calibrate your rest to the highest grade possible.

It could include:

... Doing a long walk after you finish work so that by the time you get to bed you are so tired that you sleep like a baby.

... No digital device checking after 8 PM so you avoid the white screen exposure that affects melatonin production. (Melatonin is necessary for life-affirming recovery via sleep.)

... A pre-sleep routine that includes quietly writing about the little wins of your day, noting lessons learned along with even the smallest of joyful moments, relaxing in a hot bath with soothing music, and avoiding notifications, the news and anything anxiety-inducing and overstimulating.

... Cleaning up all messes in your home spaces and setting out your exercise clothes and running shoes the night before an early morning workout (put those right by your bed) so you have zero reasons to procrastinate when you wake up.

... Resting in a cool bedroom free of technology and disturbances (use a white noise machine to block out irritating sounds if you live in a busy city).

"Sleep is God. Go worship," instructed author Jim Butcher. Words of wisdom.

32

Show Up in The Gym The Way You Wish to Show Up in Life

It's a rainy day back at the farmhouse. The windows are super old, so a little rain has seeped in, drizzling onto my beloved writing table. That's all right, though. It'll just give it more character.

My teaching within this chapter is straightforward: *Your gym routine is your life practice.* The way you show up in the fitness studio determines the way you'll operate in all other areas of your life (because the way you do one thing really is preparation for the way you'll do everything). So use your workout to set up a way of being that also serves your life well.

When I see a super-fit person, it tells me clearly that they have five key characteristics that not only serve their physical wellness but contribute to their lives as a whole:

Focus. As you work out, you're actually training your focus. Use it as a meditation of sorts, keeping your thinking on what you're doing, fully immersed in the present moment. If your mind wanders, bring it back to the now. The more you practice this, the better you'll be able to pay attention while you do any activity outside of the gym. And stay concentrated on the activities that count versus being endlessly distracted.

Dedication. The best workouts are the ones you didn't feel like doing but did—and ended up loving. Consistently doing the hard things you don't feel like doing (yet know you should do because they are so darn good for you) really is how heroes are made. So keep your self-promises and do the exercises you told yourself you would do. *Every* workout contributes to reaching your highest health goal. As you operate like this regularly, you'll notice that you'll have all-new levels of dedication and consistency that you can use to win in other areas of your life.

Excellence. Yes—this means doing the run in precise form. Performing the yoga posture with grace, skill, and calibration. Lifting the barbell with exceptionalism. Doing the sprinting nearly perfectly. Excellence in the gym is preparation for excellence at life. And ensures the making of a habit architecture within you that makes mediocrity far less likely after you've left the health club.

Persistence. I must confess to you that yesterday was one of those days in the gym where nothing really worked for me. The burpees were exhausting, the push-ups were disappointing and I felt like quitting. Yet I am not a weakling. *I do not quit.* I know that I am most alive and true to myself when I continue at the times I feel like stopping. So I pressed on. Of course, you can do this too. And when you do, you'll become so much more relentless in all dimensions of your life.

Improvement. All professional athletes are far more obsessed with the ongoing making of progress than with having the ring on their pinky finger (because they get that this is exactly how they got the ring). I watched an interview with the late NBA legend Kobe Bryant where he spoke of staying present to the process and finding joy in each and every practice session. He sounded almost like a Zen monk, preaching the benefits of living in the moment versus consistently thinking about the end result (the championship). He added that by learning to love each practice, he could do more of them than anyone else in the league: one early in the morning then another later in the morning, then another in the afternoon and yet another in the evening. With a broad smile, he concluded that by running this practice template day after day, then month after month and year after year, he increasingly built the skill and the prowess that caused him to have such a major advantage that no one else in the game could keep up with him. Ever.

So definitely do show up fully and completely when you enter your gym. Because that will set up exactly how you roll through a life filled with true wealth.

33

Become a Skilled Lifetime Multiplier

I heard a broadcaster criticizing "biohackers" and another commentator mocking the services of a European longevity clinic tucked away in the Alps. Both people said that aging is a natural and inevitable situation that humans must accept—and never play with. Really?

Makes me think of the naysayers who questioned the validity of Galileo's thesis that the Earth was round or the closed-minded cynics who said cars would never replace horses and buggies.

The hard science is clear: aging *can* be slowed by thinking, eating, and doing the right things. And some highly regarded physicians have even confirmed that aging can actually be *reversed*. Ray Kurzweil, the eminent inventor and futurist, said it smartly: "Live long enough so you can live forever." The advances in medicine and innovations for longevity coming down the pipeline will delight—and stun—you.

My wish for you in today's mentoring session is to get seriously invested in adding a few extra decades to your lifetime. Just imagine (close your eyes and do this for even a moment) adding twenty or thirty or forty or fifty (or more) *extra* years to your life by adopting lifestyle habits ranging from the sensible use of some of the revolutionary supplements available to cold plunges and ice baths, hot saunas, intermittent fasting, appropriate amounts of sunshine, an eating plan that works well for your genome, and regular meditation, along with lots of time in nature and plenty of good naps.

By multiplying your lifespan exponentially, you'll benefit mightily from the magic power of compounding, not only within your valuable financial life but in other areas as well:

... With an *extra* twenty years of life (for example) to study, practice and escalate your craft, just imagine how exceptionally superb you'll be in your profession.

... With an *extra* thirty years with your family and friends, please consider how many more adventures you'll have with your loved ones, the rich experiences you'll enjoy and the goodness you can shower on them.

... With an *extra* forty years added onto your lifespan, happily reflect on all the triumphs you can win, books you can read, travels you can take, new languages you can learn, and personal growth you will most certainly achieve.

... With an *extra* fifty more years, consider all the people you'll help, all the kindness you can show, and the magnificent impact you'll create.

Get great at multiplying the length of your life and injecting more of the extraordinary into your days. As always, start with tiny steps. Do them with consistency, and when you feel like stopping keep on walking. It's a statement of truth that we overestimate how much progress we can make in a month yet underestimate how far we can get in half a year.

Okay. SuperChum, my little dog, wants me to walk her. So I need to go. Let's talk later. Bye.

34

Go OMAD Weekly

Challenging message here. We now know that caloric restriction is good for our health and extends our lifespan. Read about *autophagy*—it'll be well worth ten minutes out of your precious life.

May I gently suggest that you fast at least once a week. Yes, once a week go OMAD: one meal a day. Even better, take the food you would have eaten on that day and give it to a homeless person or local food bank. This way, you elevate two lives. Reminds me of what Hermann Hesse wrote in *Siddhartha*, one of my favorite books: "Everyone can perform magic, everyone can reach their goals if they are able to think, if they are able to wait, if they are able to fast."

Intermittent fasting creates low-dose stress on the body, which pushes your body out of its normal state and activates what's known as *hormesis*, a phenomenon where an array of cellular processes are kickstarted that reduce inflammation, repair cellular damage, increase resilience and fight the oxidative stress, that advances aging. I usually fast two or three days a week (yet I'm not religious about this; if my body tells me it really needs to be fed, I feed it). The discipline has been life changing for my mental clarity, self-discipline, creativity, energy levels, and sensations of youthfulness.

In ancient times, the Romans, Egyptians, and Greeks used fasting to detox the body, purify their emotional lives, strengthen their fortitude, and increase their spiritual power.

Experiencing temporary hunger will also serve to raise your empathy for those in our world with empty bellies and move you to do more for those in need. So if you haven't tested this habit out, try it. It'll be hard at first. And gorgeous as it becomes your new normal.

35

Laugh More
to Live Longer

"We don't stop playing because we grow old; we grow old because we stop playing," noted Irish playwright George Bernard Shaw. Pure wisdom, isn't it?

Our world is complex, full of very real concerns and a growing array of crises. I don't want to list them as, honestly, that would hurt my heart. Anyway, one of the smartest things you can do in this confusing age is to remember the words of my great and late friend Richard Carlson: "Don't sweat the small stuff—and it's all small stuff."

Look, my steadily growing and absolutely special friend, I'm not saying that the issues our civilization is now dealing with are small. Not at all. Yet life is for the living. And—even if you're granted a long life you'll be deep under the ground, pushing up daisies, before you know it. Sorry to say it, yet connecting with your mortality every once in a while puts more vitality into your days. Because you become more conscious that they are limited.

A brilliant way to stay lighthearted in these polycrisis times is to keep your perspective. When I face a problem, I often ask myself, "Has anyone died here?" If not, I move ahead quickly and cheerfully. I also ask myself, "Will this matter in a year?" And even "What's the opportunity here?"

Then, as strange as it sounds, I force myself to laugh. I really do. Sometimes it's in the mirror and other times it's in the woods. Did you know the very act of smiling causes a cascade of neurotransmitters such as oxytocin and serotonin to be released in your brain, as well as the production of the neurotransmitter modulator brain-derived neurotropic factor (BDNF), which is a key factor in the neuroplasticity of your brain, especially for peak learning? And are you aware that laughter has been shown to reduce stress, raise your mental wellness, reduce chronic pain, improve heart health, and generate stronger immunity?

Laughter therapy has deep roots. In the 1300s, a professor of surgery named Henri de Mondeville would use humor as a tool in postoperative treatment of his patients. I smiled when I first read this. Because it's so interesting.

In 1964, Norman Cousins—a journalist—was diagnosed with a serious medical disorder. He wrote an article in the *New England Journal of Medicine* called "Anatomy of an Illness," where he reported that his recovery from degenerative collagen illness came from taking high doses of vitamin C and laughing consistently. "I made the joyous discovery that 10 minutes of genuine belly laughter had an anesthetic effect and would give me at least two hours of pain-free sleep."

To force the laughter amid his hardship, he'd watch Marx Brothers movies and *Candid Camera* re-runs and ask his nurses to read funny articles to him.

Near the end his life, Cousins noted: "It is quite possible that this treatment was a demonstration of the placebo effect. But if so, the placebo—'the doctor who resides within'—was a powerful one."

Last thing. According to one study, the average four-year-old laughs four hundred times a day while the average adult laughs fifteen times. Comedian Steve Martin would laugh for a few minutes in the mirror each morning to put himself in a positive mood. Just maybe, you should too.

36

Breathe Like a Samurai

Get this: Centuries ago in Japan, Samurai warriors tested their readiness to go into battle by having a feather placed under their nose. If the feather didn't move, they were allowed to fight. The calm breathing showed they were in a high state of focus, confidence and courage.

"To breathe properly is to live properly," taught the-greatest-of-all-time sages (yes, they were GOATs).

So many of us have forgotten how to breathe correctly, pushed by the obligations and stresses of everyday life to inhale and exhale quickly and shallowly instead of deeply, from the belly. And, via a negative feedback loop, shallow breathing sets off the sympathetic nervous system (that part of your nervous system related to the "fight, flight or freeze" response in situations of strain), generating even more stress and worry.

Breathing deeply (sometimes called diaphragmatic breathing) not only relaxes you in challenging moments and boosts mental and emotional wellness, it also optimizes your attention span (in an environment of relentless digital distraction).

The strong Samurai used breathwork as a method to lead rich, rewarding and mostly noble lives. Let us learn from them.

37

Chant Like a Monk

I am fascinated by monks and monasteries and the mental, physical, emotional, and spiritual superpowers the finest ones develop through their time-tested rituals, which range from meditation and prayer to fasting and chanting. I wrote *The Monk Who Sold His Ferrari* decades ago and yet, even before that, I was trying to figure out how these supreme souls were able to do the amazing things they do (some monks have trained themselves to raise their body temperatures at will, endure extreme amounts of pain and go on water fasts for many weeks).

One of my top fascinations with these rare-air beings is their daily practice of chanting at 5 AM and how they use this routine not only to ensure their health is ideal but also to guarantee that their spiritual lives are strong.

Science is starting to catch up with the monks and evidence is emerging that sound therapy and mantra meditation (where a word or phrase is recited repeatedly) tone the vagus nerve, which is central to stress resilience and continuous happiness.

As part of my morning practice, as the first rays of dawn present themselves, I'll often say a mantra (the "man" is Sanskrit for "mind" and the "tra" is Sanskrit for "freedom," so mantras free the mind) to set my day off on an excellent start.

My favorite slogans include:

... "Every day and in every way I'm getting stronger and stronger, healthier and happier, and kinder and kinder." (This mantra is derived from one made famous by French physician Émile Coué in his book *Self-Mastery Through Conscious Autosuggestion*.)

... "This day is a gift and I am living it beautifully, using it carefully and making steady progress confidently."

... "I am accomplishing hard projects easily and joyfully, and continuously growing in energy, mastery, and bravery."

... "To be of use, to help those in need, to do good things for as many people as I can is to live my life fully."

Hope these help! Remember, you're stronger than you know, you're more talented than you're giving yourself credit for and your future has deep magic in store for you. Trust yourself, believe in you (especially when no one else does) and keep moving ahead. Always.

38

See Solitude as a Wellness Method

We are taught from a young age to be in the company of others most of the time. Those who are alone a lot are condemned as hermits and chastised as outsiders.

Stay in the herd. Make sure you fit in. Think like everyone else. Don't dare stand out, we are schooled to think.

In so doing, we have become so separated from our most well, wise, creative, true, and peaceful selves that we don't even know what we're missing. We don't know what we don't know.

And in the rare moment that we do find ourselves in any form of solitude, we quickly reach for our drugs of choice, ranging from tech gadgets, blaring news feeds and loud music to superficial online chatting, digital dating, doom surfing, and overworking just to avoid our natural state. Of being.

Yet we are most alive in the presence of ourselves. And your relationship with you really does determine your relationship with others. You cannot be comfortable in society if you are deeply uncomfortable alone.

Practice what I call in my mentoring methodology The 3S Focus.

Concentrate often on being in Silence, seeking Stillness (in this era of hyperactivity), and enjoying the extraordinary gifts of Solitude. This trinity of states will absolutely elevate your daily experience of a wellness that knows no bounds. And the wealth money cannot buy.

"I find it wholesome to be alone the greater part of the time. To be in company, even with the best, is soon wearisome and dissipating. I love to be alone. I never found the companion that was so companionable as solitude," wrote Henry David Thoreau, one of my all-time-favorite philosophers.

And poet May Sarton observed that: "Loneliness is the poverty of self; solitude is richness of self." Good, right?

39

Supersize Your Gratefulness

As I write you this message, I'm in another part of the world where there is, sadly, much poverty. Earlier this morning I had a conversation with a man who works in the gym. I asked him how he was doing and he replied with an enormous smile (nearly the size of the Great Pyramid of Giza that we discussed in an earlier mentoring conversation) and an enthusiastic "very fine."

Then I dug deeper. He explained that he lived in "a zinc house"—that is, a small shack made of metal siding. To wash himself he'd go to a public area for water from a tap and then heat it on an old stove and bathe from a broken bucket. He had no toilet, few possessions and not much food.

To visit his wife and children, who lived in another country to save money (because it was even cheaper to live there), he softly explained that he'd have to board a bus for four days. "We almost never leave the bus during the whole trip—we're on it all day and all night. But this is the only way I can get to see my family. And we are used to it."

Then he added, still beaming—and standing quite upright with a noticeable sense of dignity (this man is a secret king to me)—"I am grateful, ever so grateful, I'm alive!"

Hmmm. Ever so grateful. Simply to be alive. May we learn from this rich-of-spirit human.

In *The Everyday Hero Manifesto* I shared a story about a man I met from a hard part of the planet who positively lit up when he saw people. I asked him why and he replied, "I've seen a lot of dead people, so when I see a live person it makes me very happy."

What marvelous, majestic, and fantastic approaches to life—at a time when too many among us, who have so much to be thankful for, grumble and complain when an airplane takeoff is delayed or the line at the grocery store is too long. Part of leading a truly wealthy life is having a generous and grateful heart, I do believe.

I know this is simple wisdom, yet I really don't see it practiced so often. Reminds me of the Persian proverb: "I cursed the fact I had no shoes, until I saw the man who had no feet."

You have a whole lot more power over how you see your life than you may currently know. One of the highest human choices is to focus on the lotus in the swamp, the roses over the thorns and the stars instead of the stones, if you get my drift.

Tonight, I feel like a very blessed man. Why? Because I'm taking my terrific daughter to dinner. No other family member, none of my friends at the table with us, not the tiny dog—just a father and his daughter. Talking about her tennis game, my recent travels, her upcoming trip to India and our latest excitements.

For this, I express immense gratefulness. On her last trip to India, my second-born brought me back a gift that she had carefully wrapped and tied with a basic yet exquisite red thread. She gave me a massive grin as she handed it to me.

"Here, Dad. I brought this all the way home, for you. I hope you like it."

I really did. And I still do. I keep that small hand-carved wooden elephant in my writing room so I see it pretty much every day. I need to tell you that it's worth more than any Ferrari (not that I've ever had one), speedboat (not that I want one) or tailored suit (not that I'd wear one) could ever mean to me. Because my daughter gave it to me.

You now know that positive psychologists use the term "deliberate gratitude" for the type of gratitude expressed by the most mentally healthy, physically hardy, emotionally happy, and spiritually strong people on the planet. It's not the once-a-year on New Year's Day kind of gratitude but appreciation as a considered, intentional, and regular practice.

The great thing about making deliberate gratitude a part of your days is that it's free. And it's easy.

Just start making a little time to be thankful for the blessings in your life. And push yourself to pay greater attention to the things that you usually take for granted. If you have eyesight, food on the table, work that helps you fulfill your responsibilities, and two feet to walk on, celebrate these gifts. You'd miss these presents if you lost them.

I'm asking you to supersize your gratefulness—beginning right now. The more you do it, the better you'll get at it (like all skills that you practice). In time, you'll earn your Masters in Astounding Gratitude and a Doctorate in Daily Delight, sensing the subtle preciousness of everything (even the hard things) that fills your world. This honestly is my prayer for you.

40

Consider That Cold Showers Decrease Doctors

Good science is confirming that "cold immersion" habits such as ice baths, swimming in a freezing lake, and frigid showers can lead to more positive moods, enhanced cognitive function and immune response, quicker recovery times after exercise, and even better cardiovascular health.

In one study published in the *European Journal of Psychology*, it was confirmed that putting yourself in 14°C (57°F) water increased dopamine (remember it's the feel-good neuroregulator that enhances focus and motivation) by 250 percent!

I need to be clear that I'm not providing any medical advice (anywhere in this book), yet research is also showing that a relatively quick cold shower has some wonderful health benefits ranging from better brain health (by the release of cold shock proteins, which protect against neuronal loss) to extended longevity (frigid water activates the proteasome to increase lifespan).

Why does it work? The answer can be found in the word I offered to you a little earlier: "hormesis." Recall this is the phenomenon where, in response to a stressful challenge on the body, a series of cellular responses are activated that serve to build strength, health, longevity, and resilience. Done in appropriate amounts, hermetic stressors such as cold temperature (or intermittent fasting, or high-intensity interval exercise) push the body to adapt, which in turn causes the formation of new mitochondria, increases removal of toxins in your system, improves blood sugar regulation, and promotes what Elissa Epel, director of the Aging, Metabolism and Emotion Center at the University of California, San Francisco, describes as "cellular housecleaning activities that slow aging."

So take more cold showers. You just might need to visit fewer doctors.

41

Exercise Your Spiritual Wellness

I'm so happy that our culture is moving forward in the understanding that peak human health is more than just being physically fit. There's an emerging and growing recognition that having a vital body is worth nothing without mental vigor and a healed emotional life.

Yet I do wish that the concept of "spiritual wellness" would seem less mysterious and mystical to most people. In my work with successful financiers, celebrity entrepreneurs, and iconic athletes, one of the learning models we start with is The 4 Interior Empires framework, which shows that world-class and highly satisfying health requires you to exercise and optimize in *four* important areas: Mindset (your psychology), Heartset (your emotionality), Healthset (your physicality), and Soulset (your spirituality). Without dedication to improvement in *each* of these realms of wellness you will never, ever be able to lead your richest and most beautiful life.

Soulset has nothing to do with religion. Not at all. Soulset training simply involves deepening your connection with your wisest self—that part of you that knows what is right for you, that stands strong and graceful in periods of trouble. That part of you that understands that to not realize your natural gifts and talents is to diminish the world (because we miss out on what your genius would produce). That part of you that is a giver versus a taker. And a hero, not a victim.

To refuel your spirit, please do make the time to be alone more often. Carve out time to sit in quietude at least a few times weekly and ideally for a profound period daily. Walk in the woods to renew your highest—and finest—self. Pray if you want to, read from the wisdom literature if you'd like to and remember to never leave the site of someone in need without doing what you can to ease their pain, in any possible way. The more people you help the more your soul will expand.

We're now at the end of the section on the second form of wealth, but I very much wish to encourage you not to neglect your spiritual life in your pursuit of top health. A well-cared-for soul will serve your life of genuine wealth so well.

THE 3RD FORM OF WEALTH

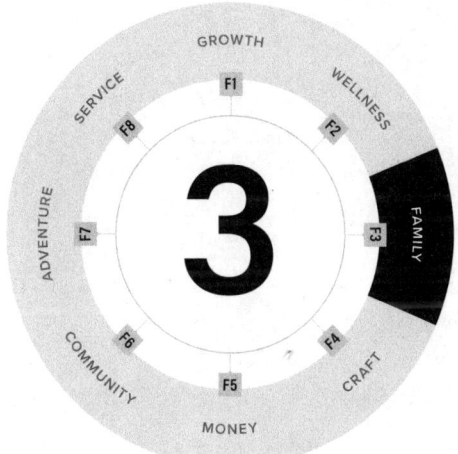

Family

The Happy Family, Happy Life Habit

A happy family is but an earlier heaven.
—George Bernard Shaw

The 3rd Form of Wealth
Family | Quick Overview

To have the love of a good (yet never perfect) family is one of life's sweetest rewards and a currency that is exponentially more valuable than any amount of money.

You can't call yourself *really* rich if you end up financially wealthy but suffer from poverty of human connections with the most important people in your universe.

A strong, joy-filled, and happy family life is a basic building block and fundamental foundation of a personal story that will not only satisfy you completely but also contain the creativity, productivity, and impact on others that the most powerful part of you seeks.

To know the caring of those who love you and to savor the companionship of good friends and well-wishers is a trophy of a genuine victory. Interestingly, too many good souls among us take their family lives for granted—until a loss happens. And only then does the vast treasure of a top home life come into sharper focus. "Love knows not its depth until the moment of parting," said the Lebanese poet Kahlil Gibran in his masterwork, *The Prophet*.

Investing in your closest relationships and enriching the hours of your days with higher love is one of the smartest and highest-yielding investments you'll ever make. So let's get going in our work together on this third—and essential—form of wealth: family.

42

That Time My Mother Took on a Motorcycle Gang

I'm not making this up: A motorcycle gang moved onto the street my parents lived on for decades. They rented a neighbor's house and would race up the street on their rides, shaking the windows of the homes on the once-peaceful, treelined suburban road in the process.

My mother—fearless as usual (she's in her eighties now)—went out and purchased a set of neon orange cones (like the ones that highway construction workers use) and carefully set them up to slow the bikers down.

She did not do this for her own benefit. She did it because my children—who were very young at the time—often played on the street in front of my mom and dad's house. And she needed to protect them (way to go, Mama Bear!).

The strategy worked—barely. The gang slowed their pace. Yet they still drove their motorcycles a little too quickly for my mother's liking.

One day, while the bikers were relaxing on their bikes outside their residence, listening to Mozart's *Jupiter* Symphony (okay, that part's not true, but all the rest is), Mom told a neighbor that she was going over.

"I'm going to have a talk with them so they slow down for my grandkids," she said. "I don't want anything to happen to the children."

"Please, no, don't go," begged the neighbor. "They're dangerous."

"I'm going," replied Mama Bear.

And, indeed, she went over. She asked them to slow down and be more careful. And to be better neighbors.

The result of her bold move? They couldn't have been more polite. Gracious, actually. This fierce and tough-looking motorcycle gang had hearts of gold. The leader said—this brings tears to my eyes as I write it—"Ma'am, your granddaughter is *our* granddaughter. We'll be very careful. Thank you."

Mom went home. She baked a gigantic batch of chocolate chip cookies. And walked them over to the crew. Seriously, she baked the bikers fresh cookies.

The leader told them that if she ever needed any help, the gang was there for her. She left with a smile. While they ate their cookies, sitting on their bikes in their driveway.

The point of the story? Easy. Few things are more important to a truly rich life than family and good neighbors. Keep yours close.

43

Create a Love Account

What small acts can you do today to deepen the bonds between you and the people you value the most? What random acts of kindness and gorgeous acts of beauty can you offer to someone in an effort to make their day just a little better? The irony of being more compassionate is that the very act of giving to others makes you feel better as well. And grows your third form of wealth, profoundly.

To practice being more loving, create a love account. Each day, make a few deposits in this very special reserve by doing something small to add joy to the life of a loved one around you. Buying your partner fresh-cut flowers for no reason at all, sending your best friend a copy of your favorite book (it better be *The 5AM Club*!), or taking the time to tell your children in no uncertain terms how you feel about them are all good places to start. (I make it a ritual to hug my children whenever I see them and whenever they leave me. Who knows what can happen tomorrow.)

Those tiny, daily deposits into the love account will give you far more happiness than a safe full of jewels. And ensure that your self-worth is always higher than your net worth (although, of course, financial freedom *is* important to your best life and I'm definitely getting to some transformational tools for how to make this real in an upcoming section that you're going to find extremely helpful). As Ralph Waldo Emerson said so eloquently, "Without the rich heart, wealth is an ugly beggar."

44

Live The Loved Ones' Eyeballs Law

Here's a top law to live if you want to have super-rich relationships with your intimate partner, family at large, and truest friends: *If something is important to them, make it important to you.*

In other words, get behind the eyeballs of that person you love. Try to see the world as they do and sense how their heart is feeling on whatever issue, activity or excitement they are sharing with you.

This idea is about so much more than general empathy. It's about significantly amplifying the importance you give to something that you might usually dismiss—because the human being that you care about so much thinks and feels it's significant.

And once you get really good at living this law, carry it out into your greater community. Live like this and your life will become a gift. And a beautiful example (to many).

45

Savor The Small Surprises of Family Life

I know this is a common idea, yet it means so much to me that I thought I'd write a short mentoring message for you on it.

Let's start with my mother again. We had a big family dinner last night and—as always—Mom asked, "What can I bring?" As usual I replied, "Nothing, Mamma—just bring you (and Dad). Everything is all handled."

When Mamma showed up, looking beautiful and elegant as always, she was clutching a little bag with something in it.

"Here, Robin, this is for you. It's fresh mint for your morning tea. I picked it up this afternoon from the market. You'll love it."

In life, it's so easy to get caught up chasing what our society tells us are the grand prizes, only to find out too late that they very much were the insignificant ones. And in life, we often forget that the seemingly small things, like my beloved mother's mint bought from a farmer's market with deep love for her son, are really the big things.

44

Live The Loved Ones' Eyeballs Law

Here's a top law to live if you want to have super-rich relationships with your intimate partner, family at large, and truest friends: *If something is important to them, make it important to you.*

In other words, get behind the eyeballs of that person you love. Try to see the world as they do and sense how their heart is feeling on whatever issue, activity or excitement they are sharing with you.

This idea is about so much more than general empathy. It's about significantly amplifying the importance you give to something that you might usually dismiss—because the human being that you care about so much thinks and feels it's significant.

And once you get really good at living this law, carry it out into your greater community. Live like this and your life will become a gift. And a beautiful example (to many).

45

Savor The Small Surprises of Family Life

I know this is a common idea, yet it means so much to me that I thought I'd write a short mentoring message for you on it.

Let's start with my mother again. We had a big family dinner last night and—as always—Mom asked, "What can I bring?" As usual I replied, "Nothing, Mamma—just bring you (and Dad). Everything is all handled."

When Mamma showed up, looking beautiful and elegant as always, she was clutching a little bag with something in it.

"Here, Robin, this is for you. It's fresh mint for your morning tea. I picked it up this afternoon from the market. You'll love it."

In life, it's so easy to get caught up chasing what our society tells us are the grand prizes, only to find out too late that they very much were the insignificant ones. And in life, we often forget that the seemingly small things, like my beloved mother's mint bought from a farmer's market with deep love for her son, are really the big things.

46

Don't Carry Grudges

Life's too short to carry a grudge. I recall reading Rolling Stones guitarist Keith Richards' autobiography, *Life*, which included a story about a time when one of his close friends stole money from him. Rather than casting the man out of his life and being bitter about it for years, the musician forgave him, thinking the friend likely needed the cash more than he did. And then he went back to his studio, to make more music.

Ninja-like, right? Zen-master-level behavior, to me at least. Such an honorable, heroic, and loving reply to the foibles of another human being.

Some people might have a completely different philosophy. "Teach them a lesson" and "No one's going to do that to me" and "They need to pay" kind of stuff. I get it. Sometimes I think like that too, I do confess.

A client recently told me that his father, sadly, was dying of stomach cancer. Had about a month left to live. The father had not spoken to his brother for fifty years. He said they had a huge fight when they were both much younger. Get this—the father couldn't even remember what the fight was about! But positions had hardened. Walls were cemented. The battle lines drawn.

And so, for *half a century*, the two brothers, once incredibly close, didn't say even a word to each other. Not one word.

. . . Think of all the fishing trips together they lost.

. . . Think of all the family meals they failed to share.

. . . Think of the laughter they didn't enjoy, the memories they didn't make and all the brotherly love they threw away.

My client said that last week the brother showed up at his father's hospital room. He just strolled in. With a card, some flowers, and a box of chocolates (wrapped carefully with a big blue bow).

The sick man said, "I'm so angry at you. For us losing all those years together." He then relaxed and coughed and began to cry.

The brother wept too, as he said, "I've really missed you." He paused, wiped away the tears and then whispered in the ear of his brother, "I love you."

My client's father passed away the next day.

Let us not carry any grudges. Nothing good ever comes from them.

47

Practice Tough Love

Relationships are *not* meant to be relentlessly hard. The first thing you want to do is get really clear on your non-negotiables and what's most important to you in a relationship. Second, it's up to you to elegantly and strictly—and sometimes toughly—protect your priorities. We really do teach people how to treat us, and if you constantly let people betray and defeat you, they will think it's okay to do this to you. And each time they do, you will lose a little more of your self-respect and personal honor.

Relationships can be hard at times, but they are not meant to be hard *all* the time. If you're in one of those bonds, you're in a toxic relationship and as your mentor from afar, I really need to tell you that you should get out (today). I know you don't think you can do better or you're praying that somehow they'll change. But a red flag is a red flag and you just might waste the greatest years of your life hoping it will turn green. Yes, you'll have to grieve your "loss" and things will be hard for a while. But the pain of heartbreak will be a whole lot easier than the tragedy of what's coming if you stay.

I'll repeat it: If you're in a relationship that's difficult *daily*, it's time for you to cut the connection. This is not a place that's good for you to be. You can do so much better. Hack the hook. Make a clean break. *Now.*

I'm certainly not saying that all relationships are super easy, or a daily walk in the park. Two human beings together is bound to bring up stuff.

I'm just saying that relationships are ultimately meant to be a source of companionship, encouragement, growth, happiness, and love. And if you don't have that, let go—so space is created for something more pleasing to enter your precious life. We both know you deserve the best.

48

Your Choice of Mate Is 90 Percent of Your Joy

I arrived at deep joy in my primary relationship fairly late in life. Just being honest. I owe this to you. Always.

In my mid-fifties, I found a true life partner. A woman who got me and vibed with me and made me feel I'd found the one I'd love to spend the rest of my years with.

I was at a place in my life where I was done with drama. Not interested in the ups and downs of intimacy that was all fire and zero stability. Been there. Done that.

We are certain to repeat the same hard experiences until we learn the lesson they arrived to teach us.

Anyway, Elle is the bomb. Beautiful, wise, articulate, beyond caring, hilarious, stylish, literate, and she absolutely shares the same core values that mean the most to me. She just sees the world the same way as I do. Fascinatingly, she grew up in the same city I did. Synchronicity is the universe's way of encouraging you quietly, yes?

Look, like I suggested in the last message, all romantic relationships can be challenging during certain periods. The chances are low that on the first or second or third one, you'll find the person who is ideal for you. As you search, please be sure to look for a partner, not a project. I believe this is an incredibly important point for everyone to remember as they choose their mates.

And yes, I do agree and acknowledge that no one is perfect. I sure am not. I've yet to meet someone with none of the flaws, scars, and strangeness that make us human. But I do believe that the right partner is out there for each one of us. As chef Julia Child once said, "The secret of a happy marriage is finding the right person. You know they're right if you love to be with them all the time." That's what I now have. And I hope the same for you (if you don't have this yet).

Oh, and once you find that person who you know is your person, fight to keep them when times get rough (they will). Amazing life partners don't grow on trees. And legendary love stories need plenty of patience.

49
—

Practice The 3 Great Friends Rule

My beloved father—who devoted fifty-four years of his life to being a community doctor—once told me, "Robin, if you have three great friends, you're a rich man. Keep your old friends close. They are great treasures—and hard to find."

To have three friends who accept you, encourage you, and love you for who you are (quirks and all) is a special gift of a life wisely lived.

> ... Friends who you can be yourself around rather than needing to pretend to be someone you're not, in order to fit in.
> ... Friends who laugh with you when you laugh, and cry with you in sorrow.
> ... Friends who get you and applaud your visions (no matter how silly they sound).
> ... Friends who you could call at 3 AM from a foreign country if you're in trouble, knowing they'd rush to the airport and board the first flight to come get you.

"Good friends, good books and a sleepy conscience: this is the ideal life," noted Mark Twain. I am certain he is right.

50

Record The Ride

I wrote about the main idea of this particular message ages ago in *Who Will Cry When You Die?* And it's worked so well in my own life that I thought I should take the insight out of the archives and share it with you today. It fits nicely into this section on the third form of wealth: family and rich relationships.

Backstory: when I was a kid, my dad took pictures of *everything*.

He loved photography—and cameras. The old kind. The type that you needed to be strong to lift and the ones that would be carried in a leather shoulder case with pockets for the various lenses to be used. The ones that are in museums of medieval history now.

Anyway. Nearly every family experience was captured on film.

. . . birthdays and graduations

. . . school concerts and vacations

. . . trips to the zoo to see the chimpanzees

. . . soaring jumps on my cheap little motocross bike (that had actually been made from a lawn mower engine)

I'll have to show you some of our family photos sometime. Yet, for now, you get the picture. Dad shot *everything*.

Snaps here and clicks there. Dad was happily and enthusiastically capturing the progress, events, and meaningful (or not) moments of the journey of our family.

It was almost *as if he didn't take anything for granted*. As if he was grateful for each thing. As if he clearly understood that family moments are fleeting. And that magic lived inside the most ordinary ones. So he revered the important ceremonies and cherished the smallest of graces. Very wise. And deeply kind. That's my dad.

One time I asked my father why he shot so many reels of photos. He just smiled. Then he placed a hand on my shoulder.

"No one knows what will happen in the future. I want to have a record of all the good things that you, your brother, your mother, and I have enjoyed together. Maybe some time ahead you and your brother will look at all the albums I've made. And feel really fortunate."

When my dad was eighty-five, at the special family dinner that Elle and I hosted before we left for Italy, he handed me a cloth bag that contained an old-school compact disc. He had taken his boatloads of photos and family movies to a shop and had *everything* put onto this disc. "All of the movies I made of your childhood are on this," he said. "It's my gift to you. Enjoy, Robin. You've been a good son to me."

I was moved. It wasn't a priceless object. But it was one of my greatest gifts.

51

Ask The 10,000 Dinners Question

One of my favorite Saturday morning rituals is to go into the city close to where we live and do a pure mobility session—to stretch and release from the intense workouts of the week that have me feeling tight. I leave renewed and completely energized. Then, I head to a marvelous square and purchase the weekend paper, which I read at a charming café (frequented by poets and artists), while sipping superstrong espresso, as the Italians around me chatter.

A while back, I read—in that coffee shop—an article about Ayesha Vardag, one of the most famous divorce lawyers in the United Kingdom. She's the one that popular footballers, renowned billionaires, and mighty royalty go to when their marriages have ended. She's been handling divorces for years and shared her insights on what makes great marriages last. "Separate bedrooms," was her first instruction. Then she continued with advice that I find to be fantastic as we work to build the third form of wealth in your life:

> The things that give you longevity in marriage are fundamentally enjoying each other's company, not just physically because that

reduces over the years. You have to have someone you have fun with, are stimulated by. You need to think in terms of 10,000 dinners: if you can imagine having dinner with someone 10,000 times, this is someone you should marry.

The people who are the happiest in their intimate relationship will tell you they "just got lucky" and that *both* of them feel like they've hit the jackpot (read that twice!). Superb relationships really are like lotteries: There's a fair amount of luck involved to win and—for those who do—there's a feeling that you've just won the big reward. That you've been blessed by The Gods of Fulfilling Relationships. And kissed by The Angels of Happiness at Home.

If you don't feel like you are beyond lucky to have the partner that you have, maybe you don't have the right partner. And, like I suggested a little earlier, it might be time for you to move on.

52

Know Opposites Don't Attract

Sure, I get the often-mentioned wisdom around opposites attracting, universes colliding, and the electricity of fire and ice mixing. Yet that just hasn't been the case for me.

In my experience, the most easy, wonderful, satisfying, and sustaining intimate relationship I've been graced to enjoy has been with an intimate partner who is a whole lot like me.

- ... We like doing the same things, so there's zero having to negotiate doing things I like to do in exchange for me having to do things I can't stand (like going on rides at amusement parks or attending sporting events with loud audiences and long games).
- ... We both adore family and spend a lot of time with ours.
- ... We are both peace lovers versus drama addicts and the few times we have a "fight," it's not anything like a real fight and it's all resolved in a few minutes. (I once read that the primary predictor of whether a relationship will last is how the couple works through conflict.)
- ... We adore each other's company, and a great Friday night is

talking for hours under the sparkling Tuscan stars, while I sip my favorite alcohol-free gin (made from botanicals) with fresh lime, a sprig of rosemary from our farm, and cold tonic water. My SuperChum Holly usually rests her head on my feet while keeping an eye open for her favorite salamander.

I need to repeat this just so I reinforce it: I have absolutely no interest in being in a romantic relationship where I spend the best hours of my finest days explaining why I have the habits I have, why I do the things I do, why I live the way I live, and why I have the urge to believe the unusual dreams I dream (like making the world better and the days of my readers brighter).

That kind of thing not only drains your life force and wastes your precious time, it creates an endless amount of misunderstanding, chaos, and general hardship (that mostly ends in disaster).

Yes, of course, please do what feels right to you. You're wiser than you know and greater than you think. Run your own race and be your own guru. I'm just doing my best to advise you on what I think will help you most.

And I do understand that—mostly—we don't choose love. Love chooses us.

And I'll definitely agree that people come into our lives for reasons, for seasons or—if you're fortunate—for a lifetime. And should a relationship end, it's not a failure, because it caused you to grow in your capacity to love. No growth in love is ever a waste.

And yet, finding someone who is *compatible* will make your life so much happier, so much more productive, fun, and tranquil. You'll experience greater creativity, dramatically heighten your productivity, make (and save) more money, enjoy far better mental, emotional, physical and spiritual health, and experience a lifestyle that you really love.

At least that's the way it's been for me.

See Little Children as Giant Gifts

One Father's Day, when my son was in elementary school, he brought home a handmade card from class. On the front of it was his small handprint and inside the card, above a little photograph of my child, were these words:

> Sometimes you get discouraged because I am so small
> And always leave fingerprints on furniture and the wall.
> But everyday I'm growing—I'll be grown up someday
> And those tiny handprints will surely fade away.
> So here's a clear one, just so you can recall
> Exactly how my fingers looked, when I was very small.
> Love, Colby

Children grow up very quickly. Life sure passes in a blink (or a wink). It seems like just yesterday that I stood in the delivery room waiting for the birth of my fine and relentlessly optimistic son and then, two years later, the birth of my wise and utterly wonderful daughter. Now they are adults. Making very meaningful lives of their own (Colby is an author and Bianca does charity work).

It's easy to promise yourself that you will spend more time with your kids when things slow down at the office or when there are fewer responsibilities on your shoulders. But if you don't act on life, life has a fascinating habit of acting on you. And the weeks really will slip into months and the months really will slip into years and the years really will slip into decades and before you know it, those little children with tiny hands who you think will remain small forever will be grown up. And gone.

54

Some Hurts Aren't Meant to Be Healed

Last night, I watched a documentary about the globally famous celebrity Pamela Anderson. It shared her experiences as an actor, her trials as an influencer, and her intense—and turbulent—love story with rock star Tommy Lee of the heavy metal band Mötley Crüe.

In one scene, Anderson is honestly and vulnerably speaking of her many marriages, unfulfilled relationships and challenges in finding a partner who was right for her. Then, while watching a video of her with Lee—during what appeared to be the best of times—she grew visibly emotional and wept, as she stood up and walked away from the camera.

The couple broke up over a quarter of a century ago. Yet it struck me as interesting—and touching—that seeing herself experiencing a magical moment with Tommy Lee still brought up such strong feelings for her. Clearly, the love she had for him never died. And seeing them together in their younger days—full of hope, promise and passion—moved her deeply. Some flames don't go out, I guess.

All I'm saying is that some hurts aren't meant to be healed and—

as strange as it seems—sometimes love doesn't die just because the relationship ends. This doesn't mean you should get back together. (It makes me think of the popular line "Sometimes people come back into our lives to see if we are still stupid.") It just means the love you shared was real and important and always to be treasured (in a secret place within your heart).

And that you're so strong and forgiving that rather than being bitter, you've remained loving. How wonderful! Bless you.

55

Do Not Be a Doormat

All right. Let us not confuse being kind to your significant other, family members, friends, or colleagues with being weak. Most gentle people have suffered a lot and overcome a ton. Their pain has introduced them to their power. They have steel on the inside.

Sometimes at the end of a mentoring session with a client, during which the discussion has centered on a relationship issue, my client will say to me: "Robin, if I'm caring and compassionate and sincere, people will take advantage of me. I don't want to be a doormat."

My reply usually goes like this: "People will only take advantage of you if you allow them to take advantage of you. You have the ability to set boundaries and to stand up for yourself. So do it. Please."

We truly do teach people how to treat us. And—in relationships—we very much get what we settle for. And receive what we accept.

The fine balance for you to master is this: Be respectful yet assertive. Polite yet brave. Civil but candid. Loving but self-respecting. Deal?

56

Know That Attachment Is Not Love

There's a giant difference between attachment and love.

Attachment is needy, clingy, and fearful. It arises from gaping wounds and childhood hurts that have yet to be healed (which is why it's essential to remedy the old cuts that have injured you so you don't pour hidden pain on people who haven't harmed you). Attachment is insecure and self-centered. It makes us do things—in relationships—that are unhealthy for us. Like being attracted to a partner who mistreats you, staying in a toxic union too long, and thinking we can't find someone better than the troubled person we are with.

Love is completely different. Love is generous and steadfast and compassionate and grateful. It makes us rise in its presence. And trust in our specialness. It's better to be alone than not to have this. I know you'll agree with me.

57

Give More Hugs

I get that you just might roll your eyes on this piece of advice. But I need to share it. Because—in reality—you'll be really happy if you live it.

First step: if you're blessed to have your mother alive (and near you) drop what you're doing (I can wait) and go hug your mama! A time will come when you can't. (Of course, do the same for your papa if you can.)

Did you know that hugging someone causes a release of dopamine, serotonin, and oxytocin in your body? Which serves to reduce your blood pressure, lower any anxiety, and promote positivity. Cool, right?

In one study of more than four hundred adults, it was discovered that the hugging habit reduced sick time; in another, embraces improved heart health. And the esteemed doctor Dean Ornish has found that people who regularly feel down, lonely and isolated are three times more likely to become ill—and die early.

So give more hugs. Your family will adore you for them and our society will be nicer because you did.

58

Turn into a People-Builder

I've been on moving sidewalks and transit shuttles that were called "people-movers." I've always found that term strange. Not sure why.

An expression that vibes with me a whole lot more is "people-builders." Shouldn't we all be one?

Should this not be one of our main aims—at home, in work, out on the streets of whatever communities we call home?

I write these sincere words to you while locked away in a hotel room in London. I am away from the noise of a very full (and sometimes weary) life spent raising family, fulfilling my ethical ambitions as an artist, and doing my best to be an instrument of service to as many people as possible, before I end up as a smoldering pile of ashes (which I hope my family will eventually cast into the ocean off the coast of breathtaking Cape Breton Island, the place where I grew up).

To shine a light on those who have no sense of their awesome talents is the work of heroes. To really, really, really care about making the people in your life bigger, better and braver is not just ever so good for the planet. It's fantastic fuel for your soul. So get great at it. Please.

59

Be a Perfect Moment Creator

Eugene O'Kelly had it all. As the worldwide CEO of accounting behemoth KPMG, he ruled over thousands of employees, was a master of his domain and had power, prestige, and prosperity.

Then one ordinary day, he attended his doctor's office to receive the results of a routine medical exam. The doctor came in with an expression you never wish to see on your doctor's face.

O'Kelly was told the grim news. He had an inoperable brain tumor. And was given ninety days to live.

Rather than complaining of and bemoaning his new reality, the executive made a dramatic decision: he would engineer the last three months of his life for genuine success in a way that was similar to how he built the global enterprise that he led.

He would live fully and meaningfully. He would repair relationships he'd broken and make the amends needed with the family he had too often neglected. He'd take the walks with his friends that he realized he'd never taken and slow down to savor life's usually unnoticed yet most valuable charms.

The leader realized that in all his years as an elite business titan, he'd never taken his wife to lunch. And on reflection, he grew aware that he'd missed many special events with his daughter, including Christmas concerts, social functions, and sporting competitions.

And so he decided to become what he called a "perfect moment creator."

With what little time remained of his once glamorous life, he would actively, skilfully, and strategically work to make memories with those he loved that were pure, wonderful, and special. Even if they were made by doing the simplest of things.

Eugene O'Kelly died a few months after that visit to his doctor. His wife posthumously published his memoir, *Chasing Daylight*, a book that has influenced me deeply. Over many, many years.

It inspired me not to put off scheduling family experiences that would bring joy to the people I adore most (I schedule family vacations a year in advance and then fit everything else around those non-negotiable events). And not to withhold the love that I had in my heart for some finer time in the future. I can't tell you how many luminaries I've advised who have told me that one of their biggest regrets is that they didn't tell a loved one how much they loved them before they passed away. Don't let that happen to you.

O'Kelly's good example moved me to take my family swimming with dolphins in Mauritius, to savor fluffy chocolate croissants with my kids in Paris (after an all-night train ride under the English Channel), to learn from an Italian chef how to make the superb *pici al pomodoro* that Colby and Bianca enjoy so much, and to spend long summer days sailing the seas without a phone, just so I could be present with the human beings I care most about.

Just think about how many words we leave unspoken, deeds we leave undone, and kindnesses we leave ungiven because we await the ideal time—one that's less hectic, more quiet and somehow more perfect.

Yet time waits for no one. Start to create perfect moments for your loved ones. Today.

60

A Gift Given to Receive Isn't a Gift

To forge more profound human connections so your life becomes more fulfilling, fantastic, and free, remember this rule: to give another person a gift with an expectation of a reward isn't really a gift—it's a trade.

The other night, I was in a restaurant enjoying a lovely meal with a group of friends. A party of tourists was seated at the table next to us.

They seemed like a large, warm, good family as they chatted and laughed. From the corner of my eye, I could see that when it came time to order the food and wine, the gentleman seated at the head of the table was unsure. So he looked over at what we were having. And then—get this—he went ahead and pretty much ordered everything that we had.

When the bottle of wine came, he looked at me with a gentle smile and said, "You seem to know what to order here so I just followed."

I grinned a very big grin. I liked him instantly and a fabulous conversation followed, ranging from his musings on his career as a marketing executive in New York City to the wonders of locally produced food, the joys that family bring, and the inspiration that modern art provides.

As the evening progressed, I asked the waiter to do me a special favor: to give my new friend a bottle of the wine that our table was sharing, as a present from me. You see, while he'd ordered the same wine as we had, the vintage we had ordered was different—and known to be that of a splendid year.

When the gift was given to him, he was *stunned*. I could see he was speechless. "Wow, thank you so much," he said tenderly. When I explained it was my pleasure, he grew emotional. And his family started to applaud. Yes, they actually *clapped* for our table's gesture.

Now here's my point: the present was given without any interest in a return. A gift given with an expectation of a reward really isn't a gift—it's a barter.

And also, kindly remember: Generosity not only makes the receiver happy. It floods you with nearly limitless joyfulness too. So both human beings prosper.

61

Other People's Bad Behavior Is Not Your Business

If someone disappoints you or otherwise hurts you, that's on them. Not on you.

They are the ones who lose reputation and personal respect and degrade their own self-love. Each time someone wrongs another they disrespect themselves, you know? At an unconscious level, their bad behavior causes their shame to grow, their feelings of unworthiness to increase, and the connection with their highest selves to further dissolve.

You didn't do anything wrong, so why should you beat yourself up about it? You're living your truth, steadfast in your values and treating people well. Good karma will be your reward and inner peace will be your repayment.

Let the wrongdoer be. And let them walk the path they are meant to walk. If you allow them to ruin your days and pollute your peace, they have won.

62

Listen Better Than You Speak

Adults are deteriorated children. As a kid, you were curious. And lived in the moment. And that made you an incredibly good listener (mostly).

Social media has trained us to become a species of broadcasters rather than receivers. Digitally, we relentlessly advertise what we're doing, share how we're looking and express what's on our minds. Me. Me. Me.

The result? In real human interactions we do the same thing. We talk more than we listen. And we focus on Me. Me. Me. How boring! And maybe even rude.

I'm in Rome, a city that makes my spirit sing, as I write today's message to you. It's December in the Eternal City, so it's cold—or at least coldish.

I'm working in bed. Country music plays in my room. The song is "Second Chance" by 49 Winchester. The vibe is good. You'd be happy, having an espresso here with me.

I'm rereading one of my favorite books from the past: *Tuesdays with Morrie*. As I read of Morrie's decency, integrity, and remarkable kindness, I feel a little sad that he's no longer around.

I pray to be even a small amount of the great man he was.

In one section, I learned that Morrie—a former university professor who loved to dance and teach his students sociology before suffering from the terrible disease of ALS—was a masterful listener.

This made me stop. And consider the power of this gorgeous habit.

To listen to another human being. Fully. Completely. Really. Truly.

We inhabit a world of humans who can't sit still. Always doing. Constantly achieving. Can't stop talking.

Yet to listen to another from the depth of your soul is to give them a blessing and—dare I say it—offer an act that is *holy*. To show someone that you care in an age of needless uncaring and to honor their presence and to confirm that they matter is an exercise in grace.

Old insight worth sharing: if we were meant to speak twice as much as we listen, we'd have been made with two mouths and one ear. Yes?

Some quick rules to become a magic-worker on the key relationship superpower of listening:

- . . . Don't interrupt others. And stop finishing their sentences for them. They are doing their best to finish them.
- . . . Know that the one who is asking the questions is the one enriching the conversation.
- . . . Trust that the person doing the listening is the person gaining the learning, so turn up your hearing.
- . . . Pause for a few seconds after the speaker has spoken to process what they have said. Too many of us are rehearsing our answer while the other is talking. Not good. Be better.

... And never, ever, never, ever check or answer your phone while a family member or friend is sitting in front of you, as it's one of the most disrespectful things a person can do.

All top communicators are spectacular listeners. And few things make a family member, friend, coworker, or total stranger feel as seen, appreciated, and applauded as being given some oh-so-uncommon listening.

Forgive me for leaving you but I need to go for a long walk to Piazza Navona and then for a three-hour lunch with my incredibly insightful, interesting, and compassionate friend Luigi. I love him a lot and I must not be late.

63

Remember That Our World Is Your Family

Maintaining your perspective is a wise move. To keep your life at its richest.

In this galaxy that we are in, did you know there are one billion other rocky planets quite similar to planet Earth? Each of these is orbiting a sun—just like our globe does.

My point? Easy, my friend. The Earth is a small place. Each of the beings on it, from various countries, cultures, creeds, and colors, is sailing through space *together* on this miraculous sphere.

We are all brothers and sisters here. Members of a tribe called People and a family called Human. When we were young, we didn't judge, resist and condemn others because they were different. No, at the playground when we'd meet a new kid we'd play easily and ten minutes later we'd introduce our parents to our new best friend.

My main point as I end our time together on the third form of wealth? We are programmed to dislike, trained to distrust, and schooled to hate. Maybe this day is the day you let down your armor a little. So more love can get in. Because on Planet Earth, our world truly is your family.

THE 4TH FORM OF WEALTH

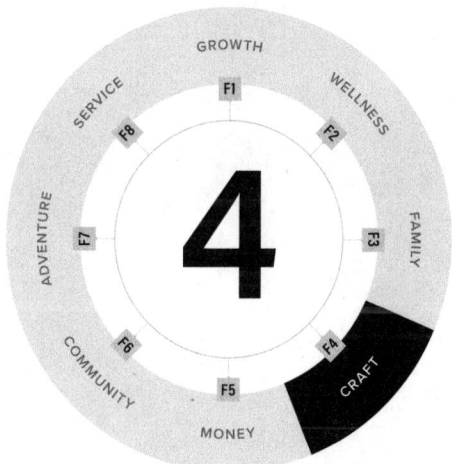

Craft

The Work as a Platform for Purpose Habit

The desire to create is one of the deepest
yearnings of the human soul.
—Dieter F. Uchtdorf

The 4th Form of Wealth
Craft | Quick Overview

One of the highest of human hungers is the need for meaning. Overwork can cause our health to fail, our relationships to fall, and our aliveness to dim, causing us to lose the essential connection with our native creativity, positivity, and sense of personal freedom. Yet a wise balance with the work that we do and a commitment to doing it as skilfully as we can—in honor of our talents and in service to delivering deep value to other human beings—is a bold and intelligent way to significantly build a life that can honestly be described as rich.

A job is only a job when seen as a job. And employment only becomes misery when you ignore the opportunity for mastery. Realizing that all work is important, all labor has deep dignity and what you do for a living can be viewed as your craft (that can introduce you to hidden personal strengths and locked-away gifts) will flood your life with far greater happiness, energy, and purpose. I really wish this for you in this era where too many good people can't stand their careers.

The majority of us see work as a ball and chain rather than as an offering and a blessing. Your occupation, in truth, serves as a chance to make the income that puts food on the family table, a possibility to make inborn potential real, a prospect to push astonishing projects into the field, and a calling to contribute to your community.

Yes, your work is an enormously valuable currency and a brilliant form of wealth that wisdom demands you value more. So let's begin exploring the awesome power of transforming your job into your craft and your labor into your art, together.

64

The Good Nun
in The Country Church

Yesterday, I walked. You know I love to walk.

Past olive groves and peaceful horses and vineyards with old vines and leaves upon them that swayed in the breeze. Past a donkey that just stared at me.

I was far into working on the manuscript of this book for you and needed a fresh place to write, aside from my usual writing room at the farmhouse. So I rented a simple room in a village near a monastery.

As I walked along the ancient and winding road, caught up in thought, I encountered a tiny stone church. It was quite marvelous, actually. I think you would have agreed if you'd been on that walk with me.

The door of the church was open, a sign of welcome. So I entered.

At the front sat a nun, playing a classical organ. She sang with sincere conviction that bordered on the glorious. And a purity that is too rare in the jaded, polarized, messy age we inhabit.

Here's the thing: the tiny stone church *was completely empty.*

Not another soul was in that place. Yet she serenaded as if she were singing for a stadium of thousands.

Alone in the church, not far from the holy sister, I sat in a pew. Closed my eyes. Listened to her enchanting song. Not making a move. Mesmerized.

I cried. Just a little. I felt alive. Elated. Even mildly favored. "Why?" you wonder.

Because of that moment. And the exquisite beauty of the scene—a human being heartfeltly showing something that spoke so intensely to me: *devotion*.

So as your gentle long-distance mentor—who really does have your back—may I humbly suggest that to reach your next level of wow as a creator and loftier heights as a craftsperson so that you rise in the fourth form of wealth, you . . .

. . . be devoted to your hopes, ideals and mighty mission.

. . . be devoted to consistency, mastery, and only what is good.

. . . be devoted to having a clean character and a rich heart.

. . . be devoted to the winning habits of champions and the daily routines of excellence.

. . . be devoted to increasing your connection with others and making them feel bigger in your presence.

. . . be devoted to doing whatever it takes to becoming supremely good at what you do for a living.

. . . be devoted to leaving the Earth better than you found it.

65

Don't Be So Logical
You Can't See The Magic

So what sort of irks me (yet not really, seriously) is when people are so caught up in their heads that they can't sense their hearts. How will you ever be able to push wonder into the world if you're blocked to experiencing what wonder feels like? Wonder is an essential part of growing your fourth form of wealth, *craft*. It really, really is.

Maybe I'm not making sense to you, so let me try again.

One of my favorite movies is *The Banshees of Inisherin* because it's so extremely hilarious, dangerous, and beautiful. And downright *magical*.

It's a film about a friend who no longer wants his best friend to be his best friend. His best friend refuses to let go. And so, the first friend starts chopping off his fingers each time his former best friend visits him. In an effort to get him to stop. Hilarious, right?

I read a review of the film that said, "I couldn't stand it because the whole thing was so unbelievable." Really? Since when does the genius of a movie depend on its believability?

What has happened to our childlike sense of playfulness, outrageousness, and marvelousness in this period of oh-so-much seriousness, scientificness (is that a word?), and mathematicalness (same?)?

The words from Steven Pressfield, the stellar author of *The War of Art*, just bubbled to the surface from my subconscious as I was writing this chapter pleading for you to not hold onto a limited creative reality too tightly:

> A child has no trouble believing the unbelievable, nor does the genius or the madman. It's only you and I, with our big brains and our tiny hearts, who doubt and overthink and hesitate.

You are a magic-worker, paid and expected and challenged (by The Giants of Your Innate Greatness) to push unusually special projects out into our tired, cynical, and unrealistically logical culture. Get your daring back. Loosen the reins that the status quo (which has sold you a philosophy on what is possible, praiseworthy and necessary) has placed on you. Dream again. Fail often. Take bold risks. Get bloodied. Then stand back up (having grown stronger and more heroic) and continue. The success of your craft depends on it.

66

The You Don't Get Lucky You Make Lucky Maxim

I was just in an interview in Dubai with Virgin Radio before writing you this message in a notebook that one of my beloved readers handed to me as a gift at a book signing. The utterly splendid interviewer, who was most kind to me, asked, "Robin, does everything happen by luck or is it what we do that makes the luck?"

"Yes." That was my answer. Just "yes."

Meaning, it's both. I do very much believe in APR: *Absolute Personal Responsibility*. We must rise early, develop our strongest and bravest selves, keep our promises. We need to work hard at work (too many people are faking it at work yet wishing for top results: that won't work), deliver superior value to those who count on us, be encouraging to our family, make time for healthy recreation, and do our part to have a positive impact. All of these are keys to worldly winning.

Good things happen to people who do good things. Especially to those who wholeheartedly do their jobs like they really care and are devoted to making a difference—even and especially when everyone around them is a checked-out cyberzombie escaping into the digital universe instead of being right here, right now. You see, my friend, we don't really get lucky—we make lucky. You have such a large part to play in how your life turns out!

Having said this, I do also believe in destiny. I think that a set of invisible hands guides our journey, is behind instances of synchronicity, and protects us during periods of adversity. That's just my belief—it may not be yours, and that's just fine with me.

My sense is that heaven helps those who help themselves. Do your best *and then* let life do the rest is what I'm really trying to remind you of, with love and respect.

Should something not work out (like losing a job or ending a relationship), please don't fall into the trap of self-deception. Don't CBE: Complain, Blame and Excuse. Instead, take an honest, hard look at your part in the loss. And improve what needs to improve so it doesn't keep happening. That's APR. And part of being a high-functioning, honestly rich human being.

You don't want to be like that person who keeps stumbling through relationship after relationship and saying, "Why aren't there any outstanding people out there for me?"

Having reinforced the importance of APR, once you've looked in the mirror and taken deep accountability for your piece in the outcome, *let go*. And *trust* that if you were meant to be—in your best interests—where you wished you'd be, then you'd be there, if you get my drift? And if you're not where you hoped to be, something even better is in the cards for you.

Exercise your inherent wisdom to know that a failure is only a failure when seen as a failure. Every so-called failure carries a secret fortune, just begging you to pay attention to it.

I've grown the most from my most tragic experiences. While enduring them, I wished they would end. Now—after time has passed—I see that they arrived to serve me so well. To help dissolve my ego, raise my wisdom, build intimacy with my gifts and open my heart to greater love. I encourage you not to waste a difficult time. Actually, as strange as it sounds, stay in it as long as possible because the growth you can get from it is priceless.

And, on reflection, I really am grateful that I didn't get everything I wanted. Because where life was leading ended up being vastly brighter. The same holds true for you.

67

Start a Stop Doing List

Most of us have a To Do List. When I was a young litigation lawyer, I actually ran my entire life by one. Everything was written down and I lived off this list with military-grade precision. It wasn't much fun. But I did get a lot done.

The To Do List that so many of us keep often contains our work commitments, team meetings, bill payments, grocery items, and social events.

That's fine. Good, actually. Keep it going if it serves you well. And yet, I'd like to tell you about something I now do differently, which serves me nicely: a *Stop Doing List*. You see, a great and sweet life (and career) is so much more about what you choose to *stop* doing than what you vowed to start doing.

Your list might include the decision to:

... Stop comparing your real life to the fake lives manufactured (with filters and all) online.

... Stop buying so many things you really don't need, understanding that being frugal is super smart in a time of influencers encouraging you to eat in expensive restaurants, purchase luxury clothes, and fly to places they really can't afford.

- ... Stop accepting every social invitation that comes your way because you have a deep-seated addiction to being liked.
- ... Stop stressing about problems that are not real and worrying about things that will probably never happen. "Remember, today is the tomorrow you worried about yesterday," said Dale Carnegie.
- ... Stop complaining about how impossible that assignment you're working on is and start getting the work done. (One step at a time is how masterpieces are made; remember the Great Pyramid of Giza earlier in our work together?)
- ... Stop saying yes to business opportunities that you really should say no to.
- ... Stop spending the prime hours of your days engaging in superficial distractions and digital diversions.
- ... Stop giving anything less than your finest effort in everything you do at your job.
- ... Stop following the pack and start leading the field.
- ... Stop scrolling when it's time to be creating and stop chit-chatting when it's time to be producing.

You have only *this* life to live. Your happiness, healthiness, greatness, and wealthiness depend on using your days well. So shift from focusing mostly on the things you need to do into a clearer and more concentrated sense of what you need to strip out of your hours. Mastery is far more about the pursuit of simplicity than the seduction of complexity. And a meaningful and satisfying life is sometimes more about what you take out of it than what you put into it.

68

Avoid The "No One Will Notice It" Lie

Steve Jobs's real hero was his adoptive father, a remarkably great craftsman who sweated every detail to make perfectly formed furniture in his free time. As a boy, Jobs would watch him measure the wood with fierce precision, line up the corners with near obsession, and be monomaniacally focused on getting the job done at a world-class level.

One day, his father instructed him to go paint the fence outside their home and he did as told. A few hours later, his father appeared. "Steve, did you paint the fence?"

"I did, Dad, look," the young Jobs replied, pointing to the structure. His father carefully inspected the work then observed, "Steve you've done a nice job painting the outside of the fence, but you didn't paint the *inside* of the fence."

Steve responded, "But, Dad, no one will see the inside of the fence."

His father smiled, paused and then said, "But, Son, *we* will."

Many years later, Jobs was working with his design team on the first Apple Macintosh. His instruction to his group? Make the computer beautiful on the outside. Make it look special, wonderful, and sensational. But the real mission, he pronounced, was to make the *inside* of the machine a work of art.

Someone on the team mused, "But, Steve, no one will see the inside of the computer." And, of course, Jobs paused and then replied: "But we will."

You see, whatever you do at work, the bravest and sagest part of you sees *everything*—and I do mean *everything*—you do. And each time you betray your greatness by doing something that you know disrespects your genius, a small part of you dies. Part of you loses self-respect. Part of your enthusiasm, optimism, and hopefulness leaves you. Each act of average causes your promise to become defeated. And potential unexpressed turns to pain.

So when you feel like playing small with your gifts or going minuscule with your personal magic, just remember that someone is always watching you. And that someone is always your highest you.

69

Bring a Security Guard to Work

On a podcast I heard a while ago, I learned author Neil Strauss has a quirky yet creative practice designed to ensure he gets a big project done. He hires a security guard with the instruction to stand outside of his home and not—under any condition—let him leave until his book is completed.

You can have fun all the time or realize your personal potential. It's not really possible to have both, is it?

Like Strauss, you absolutely must develop strategies and protocols that force you to finish the work you know you must finish to lead your field and to make the world a friendlier place, because you've pushed your artistry into it.

You might not bring a security guard to work. But you really should do something dramatic to complete your most valuable project.

Before the opportunity to get it done is gone.

70

Use The Virtuoso Algorithm

If you were sitting in front of me and asked me to summarize in a simple formula what makes the greatest CEOs, billionaires, entrepreneurs, professional athletes, and leadership teams great, here's what I'd offer:

$$\frac{\text{GROWTH} \times \text{PRACTICE} \times \text{TEACHERS} \times \text{ASSOCIATIONS}}{\text{RESILENCE} + \text{LONGEVITY}} = \text{MASTERY}$$

Yes, that's exactly what I'd draw for you on a napkin.

"Growth" means that you must study and refine your craft more than average performers in your domain, so you have the *insight* to do purely what the best do.

"Practice" in the equation is obviously about putting in the training hours so you get the mileage required to capitalize on making your inborn talents into outer genius.

"Teachers" is a code word for securing terrific mentors who

help you steadily improve your skill of focus and save you years of time wasted doing the wrong things.

And "Associations" refers to the humans you hang with. Spend most of your days with those who are devoted to becoming supreme in their field and their energy, mastery, audacity, and work ethic will rub off on you.

The denominator in the formula has two important words in it that I'd invite you to consider. "Resilience" is the trait of turning failure into fuel and stumbling blocks into stepping stones. Most performers give up quickly, so they get zero traction around their inspiring vision. Fortune favors the relentless. Remember that.

And "Longevity" is the basic yet important idea that unusual success comes by staying in the game longer than the world tells you is reasonable, responsible and rational. To get to BIW (Best in World), you must outlive your peers. And the key to becoming legendary is extending your lifespan within your domain.

My final thought in this message is reinforcement to trust the quiet whispers that come to you in the most unexpected moments, instructing you on the enterprise that you must pursue to discover the height of the powers that light you up. This is the very project that, once done with concentration, carefulness, and courage, will also light up the world.

"A person should learn to detect and watch that gleam of light which flashes across their mind from within, more than the luster of the firmament of bards and sages. Yet we dismiss without notice our thought, because it is ours. In every work of genius we recognize our own rejected thoughts: they come back to us with a certain alienated majesty," wrote the mighty philosopher Ralph Waldo Emerson.

Take five minutes, now, and reflect on these words. Your intuition is extraordinary, and your insights are strong. Ignore the haters and overlook the critics. Advance your virtuosity and you're bound to experience the joys, satisfactions, and generally untalked-about treasures of treating your job as a craft, the fourth form of wealth.

71

Learning Is Your Superpower

A closed mind never raises the world. And an exceptional performer who stops consistently growing, optimizing, and evolving in their area of expertise is declining, often without knowing (until it's too late). Which brings us to the mission-essential power of learning.

Education is inoculation against disruption. And the creative producer who learns the most, wins.

For many years, I've taught a primary principle to my billionaire, CEO and movement-maker clients known as *The 2x3x Mindset*. It will help you upgrade your dominance in any field you may wish to lead. Here it is: To double your income and your impact, *triple* your investment in two core areas—your personal mastery and your professional capability.

Too many good people are suffering from the restricted belief that genius is a divine gift rather than a daily practice. It took Mozart ten years of focus, training, and persistence before the *first* signs of his mastery revealed themselves. Jane Goodall, the revered primate scientist, studied chimpanzees for decades before she truly expressed her exceptionalism. Einstein worked as a postal clerk and struggled in anonymity for years before arriving at the General Theory of Relativity, which revolutionized the understanding of physics. Aristotle Onassis arrived in Buenos Aires, after a treacherous voyage from Greece on an ocean liner, with only $60 in his pocket before embarking on the long journey of building the enterprises and entrepreneurial powers that made him the financially richest entrepreneur of his day.

Each of these people started small, *learned* what they needed to learn to win and never, ever stopped improving their art. As simple as it sounds, their winning formula was that they always wanted to get better, through self-education.

And definitely understand that if you think "I can't become a force in my field," or "Superstars are made of stardust different from mine," or "The best are blessed with rare talents I just don't have," rather than knowing that genius within a craft is born from a marvelous alchemy of focus, learning, training, mentorship, execution, persistence, and the passage of time, then that flawed thinking will eventually wire into a limiting subconscious belief. In other words, if you're telling yourself a psychological story that says, "I am average, so I must operate at ordinary," that will manifest as your reality. *Because your daily behavior always reflects your deepest beliefs.*

Restricted thinking always creates a faulty program that writes a story that then becomes your self-identity. This, in turn, determines how you show up each day. Yes, your thinking is a self-fulfilling prophecy. And what you believe about your potential becomes real.

The respected psychologist Carol Dweck has found, through her rigorous research, that world-class performers have "a growth mindset," rather than a fixed one. In other words, they see opportunity in such a way that, if they don't have a skill, they understand they can learn it. And if they want to master a subject, they get that deep practice and concentrated effort will help them own it.

Those who *choose* to operate via a growth mindset have agency over their lives and a closely held appreciation that *all* human beings have the power to get better, each day. By learning what they must and then doing what's needed to improve, versus waiting for the stars to align.

Study. Study. Study. And read, read, read! I know of few other investments that give you the exponential rate of return that a great book does. For a few dollars, you can get into the minds of the greatest people who have lived. You can discover their philosophies, embrace their daily habits, understand how they handcrafted their masterworks, discover how they overcame adversity, and grow inspired by their paths.

The victim says elite performance is too hard and so wastes precious hours in front of their big TV. The superstar gets that mastery takes study, effort, patience, and dedication. And spends a ton of time building a large library.

"In my whole life, I have known no wise people who didn't read all the time—none, zero," remarked fabled investor (and Warren Buffett's business partner) Charlie Munger. Beautiful, right?

72

Develop a Lust for Books

Sorry, but I will not stop encouraging you to read more books. Because I want you to fill your mind and heart and home with them. To be surrounded by wisdom—by having stacks of texts (yes, I like the paper ones best)—is one of the best things in life. At least for me. And I'm pretty sure for you.

Here's a quick list of a few of the reasons to read for at least an hour every day (for the remainder of your life):

Reason #1: Reading—in an age of online algorithms feeding you information and media bias—allows you to make the revolutionary step of thinking for yourself. By consuming content from many authors—of different opinions—you can form *your own* conclusions on the topics that matter. And avoid operating in an echo chamber.

Reason #2: Reading helps you go deep in a culture gone light. Rather than digital snacking on information through one-line messages and ten-second videos, immersing yourself in a book (especially a hard one to read) builds the muscles that make you a heavyweight thinker. And this ability, in turn, will allow you the

GCA (Gargantuan Competitive Advantage) of being one of the rare-air few who have the mental toughness to solve difficult problems.

Reason #3: Reading lengthens your attention span in an environment where the majority suffers from the profound weakness of not being able to focus. All geniuses have built supreme levels of concentration—which causes them to regularly enter the flow state for endless hours where they access the near-magical ideas that eventually make them legendary.

Reason #4: Reading raises your knowledge base, which aids you in pushing more magic into the marketplace. Growing in insight also reduces the number of mistakes you'll make as you leverage the wisdom of the giants you study. This means less wasted time, less personal pain, and a whole lot less hardship.

Reason #5: Reading elevates your inspiration. You can't inspire your followers, customers, and industry if your own well of inspiration is empty. A superb way to stay optimistic, enthusiastic, and overflowing with contagious positive energy is to read works of heroic exploits. Read the biographies of adventurers who scaled the highest summits and explored desolate deserts. Study the autobiographies of the inventors who overcame the odds and entrepreneurs who transcended common limits. Associate with the great men and women of history who freed captive nations, launched global movements, and represented the best humanity has to offer by reading of their lives, by moving through their books.

I could list many more reasons that I want you to read everything you can get your hands on and turn pages instead of watching amusing videos (that often leave you feeling intellectually emptier and spiritually poorer than before you began).

I'll say it again because I really care about your rise: Read daily! Read daily! Read daily!

73
—

Live The Grandmaster Beginner Law

Before sitting down to write this mentoring message to you in my messy writing room, I walked on a new trail in the woods with SuperChum. Amazingly, a white-tailed doe jumped out of the trees and sprang across my path. It was magical! A sign of some sort?

Anyway. Enough of that. Let's jump right into the lesson I wish to share with you today so your positivity, productivity, leadership, and service to society can soar.

And here it is: *The thing about great masters is that they always think like beginners.*

That's a good mantra to meditate on, write about, and work thoughtfully around.

Too many superproducers and top performers reach the peak and then start thinking they know it all or are invincible and can never be knocked off their lofty perch. And of course, this mentality is the start of the end. Because mastery without humility breeds mediocrity.

Kobe Bryant, at the height of his powers and peak of his prowess, used to show up at the gym at dawn. No excuses. No complaints. No rationalizations for skipping the training because he was a superstar and could do whatever he wished.

Although he was a master, he behaved like a beginner, hungry to learn, obsessed with improvement, and fanatical about growth.

In the fascinating documentary *The Redeem Team*, one Team USA basketball player recounts how he and his teammates partied all night in a club, enjoying themselves in the foreign city they were in.

He then recalled that on entering the lobby of their hotel, they saw Kobe in full gym gear. Holding a bag with his weightlifting gloves. Sweat pouring down his face from an early morning workout. Staring at them. *Intensely*.

It was 4 AM. (I guess The 5 AM Club started too late for him.)

The example set by Kobe that day affected the entire team. His commitment became contagious.

Many talked about what they had seen that morning for days afterward, speaking about Kobe Bryant's dedication, fierce love of the game, and ferocious desire to win the Olympic gold medal.

And guess what?

By the end of the week, the entire team had become mesmerized by his devotion. They were in the gym just past daybreak, doing the work required to reach the goal they wanted (which they did).

What I'm suggesting, with much love and respect, is this ...

... The moment you think you're untouchable, you're in decay.

... The minute you take your success for granted is the moment you must refocus on iterating your craft, upgrading your skill, and optimizing the performance that will take you to even higher reaches.

... The instant you stop rising early, putting in the practice, investing in your learning, pushing greater, and doing whatever it takes to impress all witnesses (and honor your natural promise) is the day you step onto the path of irrelevance and go down the road to obsolescence.

Years ago, I was invited to speak at a leadership conference with the illustrious business titan Jack Welch of GE. Interestingly, he wasn't in the green room all day, hobnobbing with the celebrities or sipping champagne in the VIP lounge while chatting with influencers. No—not at all.

For the entire event, he was in the front row, taking notes on everything that I and the other speakers on the bill had to say. He understood that the moment you see yourself as an expert, you think you've heard it all before and then close yourself off from learning new ideas (and developing next-level skills). Because you've fallen into the death spiral of thinking you know it all.

His behavior revealed the humility that sustains the mastery that eventually breeds immortality. Which is my humble prayer for you.

74

Make Your Project X

The Taj Mahal. Pavarotti's "Nessun Dorma." A meal at Cal Xim in Penedès. *The Birth of Venus* by painter Sandro Botticelli. The secret communication system invented by Hedy Lamarr. The design of AC electrical current by Nikola Tesla. "Bohemian Rhapsody" by rock group Queen. The Acropolis in Athens and the Colosseum in Rome.

All masterworks testifying to the ingenuity—and expertise—of human beings standing for possibility and craft excellence in a time of increasing mundanity. (When was the last time you spotted magic in the marketplace?)

I recall taking my mother to the Galleria dell'Accademia in Florence. Her face on walking into the main room and seeing Michelangelo's *David* can never be erased from my memory. Mom was enchanted. By the beauty, skill and scale of the masterpiece.

All I'm suggesting to you here is that you become one of those rare and remarkable producers who refuse to chase every shiny opportunity and have the discipline (and guts) to focus on a *single* work that, when refined, calibrated, polished, optimized and then nearly perfected (even if it takes ages to get the gorgeous thing done), makes the jaws of the world drop.

Each of us has within us a magnum opus. A grand and glorious venture that—on the thought of it—fills us with excitement, enchantment, and the richly felt sense that our lives matter.

Yes, do *your* Project X.

Your Eiffel Tower. Your *Mona Lisa*. Your Theory of Relativity. Your penicillin. Your Concorde. Your Empire State Building. Your *Guernica*. Your *Titanic*. (Okay, maybe the last one isn't the best idea. Yet you get my point.)

I feel we are steadily growing as friends. And friends are candid with each other. And so, I must say this to you: *Nothing is so heartbreaking as getting to your end with your magnificence frozen within you.*

To live your richest life, you really must do some soul-searching (now!) and start the process of discovering the *one* enterprise that—even if it takes a lifetime to complete—will stand as your monument to the best creativity, highest productivity, and outright poetry within you. Not one hundred projects. Not fifty. Not twenty. Nope. What's the *one* initiative that your heart has been telling you that you need to do to honestly honor the greatness within?

And once you figure it out, begin it. Immediately.

75

Hard Work Is Great Work

The venture you're most resisting is the one you most need to start doing.

All too often, we think that the project that terrifies us is the one to avoid. No. That's the one to *accept*. Because the fears we don't face become our walls. And the opportunities we run away from rob us of our genius.

As well, remember that the hardest work ends up being the highest fuel for our satisfaction. It's such a paradox, right? Yet the truth really is that by the consistent doing of difficult things you'll build intimacy with the brilliance, strongness, and goodness that currently await untapped within you. Getting to know these usually invisible parts brings lasting joy. Knowledge of our heroic selves brings huge happiness. And in the solving of tough problems, fulfilment, meaning, and purpose become our constant companions. This is why I say that courageously pursuing (and pushing) your craft is a form of wealth. And an incredible source of riches in your life.

In some circles these days, hard work has a bad name. Sure, we must rest, recover and enjoy the fruits of our labor. Yet going all in on the professional pursuits you choose to commit to will bring immense energy, confidence, enthusiasm, and peacefulness to your days. The habit of working really hard works really well. It'll give you a giant advantage over all the people who say they want a rich life yet won't do anything to make one. And make your life so much more special.

76

First Drafts Are Meant to Be Bad

Ernest Hemingway said something that has helped me enormously as an artist always working to improve my craft: "The first draft of anything is sh*t."

Now, I don't like foul words, yet I need to accurately quote what he wrote. And the insight behind what he said is monumentally important for us to understand.

When I work on a book, I rush to get the initial manuscript done. I don't worry much about spelling or technique or finding the perfect calibration of words. Instead, I just push to get the main ideas down.

This, then, gives me the feeling the work is mostly done even though it's just the beginning. Psychologically it makes me feel like the heavy lifting is over, even though it's not. Then, on the next drafts, I cut and rework and replace and polish (over and over and over again).

In *Bird by Bird*, writer Anne Lamott tells the story of her father's advice to her brother, who was finding it hard to finish a project on birds. Just take it "bird by bird" was the advice. Nice.

Lamott also said that first drafts are meant to be bad. Remember this. Quickly produce the earliest version of your Project X. It'll give you momentum—and the feeling most of the drudgery is done. Then, take it page by page, brushstroke by brushstroke, bird by bird. If you know what I mean.

On each draft that follows, add and subtract. Improve and iterate. Keep making the continuous and tiniest of changes that move the work from the mundane toward the masterful. Until you arrive at the finest result you have inside of you to send out into a universe craving your magic.

77

Stop Copying Your Heroes

"I don't care that they stole my idea. I care that they don't have any of their own," the world-changing inventor Nikola Tesla once stated. He deserves far more credit for his ideas and creations than he currently receives, by the way. Because he was a better thinker than promoter, others less brilliant have become more prominent.

Anyway, what I'd love for you to think about as you scale your creativity, upgrade your productivity, and calibrate your craft toward increasing the fourth form of wealth in your life is the uncommon display of originality.

Here's an important maxim to tattoo onto your brain: *You can copy your heroes or you can influence your industry, but you'll never be able to do both.*

Often people copy because they are in scarcity. They are scared because they don't think they have enough creativity to allow them to win. So they take the easy way out—and steal the ideas of others. Or they are so disconnected from the imagination and talent that lie at their core, they ignore the instructions their muse is offering them.

Another key concept: The marketplace rewards the delivery of *original* magic. (Stop reading and write this line in your journal a few times so it drops deeper into your understanding.)

Tesla and Gaga. Da Vinci and Jobs. Ali and Jordan. Dickinson and Einstein. They all have one thing in common: they brought *fresh* value to their area of influence. Rather than following the herd, thinking like the majority, and passively fitting in, they stood out, got really, really, really good at their craft and then shared their virtuosity with many.

Oh, and once you start releasing originality, innovation, and breathtakingly great invention into your field, know and trust that the marketplace will reply with what I call in my mentoring methodology The 3 Rewards of Mastery:

Reward #1: *Income.* Inspire, delight, and serve more people and you'll receive a larger paycheck. Because money is a by-product of problems solved and helpfulness rendered.

Reward #2: *Influence.* The more you have the focus, wisdom, and execution ability to bring your natural genius into the light of day, the more people will appreciate and applaud your expertise. That brings you the second reward of mastery—power. And the result of influence.

Reward #3: *Freedom.* Yes, the third gift you're bound to get on becoming a virtuoso is the freedom that flows as your income grows and your influence expands. You'll be able to do whatever you want to do, with whomever you want to do it, whenever you wish to do it.

The main idea for you to embrace before I leave you here and begin to cook a pasta dinner with fresh basil, ripe tomatoes from our farm, and olive oil so splendid it makes me want to sing from the treetops? Stop copying your heroes. No one on the planet today can create, deliver and operate quite the same way as you. So rather than working hard to be the second-best version of someone you admire, may I politely suggest you invest your finest work hours in becoming the single greatest vision of yourself.

78

Just Be Friendly

Winning at work is so easy because there are so few people doing the things that lead to winning at work these days.

Success lies in a masterful consistency around the fundamentals. And too few are very good at the basics, like doing your job with a sense of pride, care, and friendliness for others. Here's an example to make my point. Maybe with a little humor.

I was in a big North American city, out for a long walk in the rain (walking in the rain is one of my favorite things).

As I walked, I spotted a small shop that advertised coffee with adaptogens—substances that boost brain focus, memory, energy, and hardiness against the toxic results of unmanaged stress. I was fascinated by the way everything was branded and packaged. So I entered.

The young hipster with a cool hat behind the counter didn't say a word. Just looked at me blankly and then went back to his phone. The place was pretty much empty, yet he didn't seem happy to see me.

No sweat. I smiled. And said "Hi." He grunted a greeting, as people who spend too much time in online pursuits usually do because they no longer know how to connect with other humans. And have forgotten the sweetness of this particular habit. And have lost sight of what most matters to a life richly led.

I studied the products. They looked amazing. The founder of the firm had clearly invested a lot of thinking (and money) in creating excellent goods that would help people perform at their best.

I asked the young man if this was a chain or a single shop.

"Single," he said, as cold as an ice bath. Then he swayed his body to the hipster music he was playing. I'm serious. He did some freaky moves to the music instead of taking my question seriously. I wish you'd been there with me. You would have found the dancing quirky too.

I asked if the supplements came in smaller packages that I could take home rather than simply being consumed at the shop, mixed with the coffee they made there.

"No, we used to have little packages but not anymore," he replied, not looking up from his fully loaded phone.

Another freaky dance move like an otherworldly robot. Then a "tap tap tap" on the device with his finger, checking something that was clearly far more urgent than me.

To be present to another person. To give a human the stellar gift of even the mildest of exuberance on greeting them. To display fluent product knowledge, along with unusual expertise when helping them. And to show sincere dedication to making the days of others happier is how you discover victory at work, while calibrating your craft. And raise your own self-respect, inspiration, career, and lifestyle in the mix. How easy it is to forget this! Just do the basics and focus on the fundamentals. Because so few are doing them anymore.

Whenever you're wondering how you should show up when you're with a customer, teammate, supplier or other individual standing before you, remember the hipster with the very strange dance moves. The one with the cool hat.

And just be friendly.

79

Set Your Daily 5

A productivity protocol that the clients I advise have found exceedingly useful is The Daily 5. It's pretty simple—like all valuable tools. Each day, simply set five tiny triumphs, little wins or granular goals that you promise yourself you will get done before the day ends. Because as you now know well: *Small, daily, seemingly insignificant improvements, when done consistently over time, lead to stunning results*. And it's not what you do once in a while that will get you to great, but what you do every day.

No matter what's on your plate and how your life is currently running, you can *definitely* get five microvictories done.

Examples of easy things to do include:

. . . Make your bed as soon as you get up.
. . . Do twenty push-ups after you brush your teeth.
. . . Do a fifteen-minute meditation before breakfast.
. . . Skip breakfast and fast for a few hours.
. . . Write a few things you're grateful for in your morning journal.
. . . Prepare a love letter to your partner.
. . . Spend the first hour of work on real work versus busy work.
. . . Send a handwritten thank you note to someone who has helped your progress.

... Watch a learning video that will optimize your top skill.
... Spend an hour on the project that will most promote your career.
... Find something encouraging to say to a teammate.
... Notice something in your day that makes you feel more alive and savor it.
... Do something kind for a stranger on the street.
... Have a family meal free of technology.
... Write three things you're grateful for before you go to sleep.

Here's the powerful point I want you to play with: five granular wins done each day become one hundred and fifty in just a month and eighteen hundred improvements in just one year. The coming twelve months are absolutely certain to become the most productive, successful, and phenomenal twelve months of your life (yet) as you make eighteen hundred tiny goals real.

80

Think Like an Artist

I adore the artwork of the American maestro Jean-Michel Basquiat. I'm a massive fan of the abstract painting of Austrian luminary Martha Jungwirth. I can stare at a portrait created by the modern-day South African master Lionel Smit in a gallery for hours and hours, losing myself in his brilliance.

Art, to me, makes life more beautiful, easier and better. It makes dull days brighter. And when I am in the presence of artistic greatness, just a little of their giftedness rubs off on me. Leaving my craft a bit higher.

Okay. *Think Like an Artist*. This is the instruction, and the request, that I have of you. No matter what you do for work, you are a creative. And what you produce (whether it's pizza or screenplays, companies or code, start-ups or spin classes) is your precious art. Your good name is on it. So make what you make extraordinary. Otherwise, don't do it.

Four practical lessons to encourage you here:

Lesson #1: Make the work you produce today better than yesterday's output and the work you do this year exponentially better than that of the last one.

Lesson #2: Care more about quality than anyone in your industry. Mastery or nothing! Know that *excellence is an energy*. People can feel it without you having to say it. We can all sense when we are in the company of greatness.

Lesson #3: Exploit your strangeness and mine your oddness. The weird things about you are the very things that can make your native genius real. Think through, journal about, and meditate upon the unique quirks, talents, and strengths that set you apart from everyone else. Then, develop and amplify them.

Lesson #4: Trust that mistakes are the gateway into artistry, and failure is the price your talent must pay to fully express itself. Use your errors, setbacks, and messes as fuel for artistic power. As Nietzsche said, "Chaos gives birth to dancing stars."

Live out on the skinny branch (it's dangerous on the limb but that's where all the fruit is!). Take more creative risks. Don't be afraid to look foolish, and always remember that no one takes seriously the person who takes themselves too seriously.

Think like an artist. Because you are one.

81

Find Your Personal Goldeneye

To produce your masterwork, you need to be alone a lot. I'm not saying working with a team isn't important or helpful. The bigger the dream, the more essential the team. And as I've said earlier, a profound connection with family and friends is an essential foundation for genuine success.

Having noted this, my real point here is that in a time of extreme technological stimulation, hyperdistraction, and cognitive overload, you really, really, really need to *force* yourself to get away from your usual life on a regular basis to do world-class work, even if that's only for a few hours each day.

All artists have studios where they retreat daily. All scientists have their labs where they labor and conduct experiments. All pro athletes have their gyms. And all legendary musicians have their practice rooms.

"All medicine men live in caves," observed artist Jean-Michel Basquiat. To me, that means you can be in the noise of the world or make your masterpieces through being alone—but never both. Your genius is begging you for more silence, solitude, and stillness. And all multiple-masterwork-makers understand that where you work profoundly shapes the quality of the work—so they place themselves in scenes that inspire their most monumental productivity.

Ian Fleming, the famous writer of the James Bond novels, purchased a marvelous cottage on the ocean in Jamaica where he would go to find quietude and generate the all-important flow state to create the stories that have entertained millions. He called his place Goldeneye.

If this major performer gained such inspiration, execution energy and productivity to complete his extraordinary body of work by getting away from the loudness of society, shouldn't you find your Goldeneye too?

82

Go The Extra Mile

When I was writing *The 5AM Club* (it took me four full years to get it done, and getting that book to the absolute best I could make it became a mission that bordered on an obsession), I traveled by train to a small European town and found a hotel to stay in for a week to write. I made more progress on the manuscript in that one week than I'd made in the previous month of working at home.

On that trip, someone from room service provided my morning lemon tea with a curious feature I've never forgotten: the lemon halves had the seeds carved out of them.

I'm not sure if I'm being clear here, so allow me to be clearer: rather than simply cutting the lemon in half so I could squeeze the juice into the hot water, some dedicated soul had taken the time and gone to the trouble to carefully cut the seeds out so they wouldn't fall into my tea.

I was so impressed by this unusual act of unexpected excellence that I mentioned it in the book. I called the concept Deseeding the Lemon Wedges, a metaphor for showing the painstaking attention to detail that is the bedrock of becoming a master of your craft.

As I write you today's mentoring message, I'm back at the same hotel. And guess what? I have a new metaphor for you, based on today's cup of tea.

I ordered fresh mint tea. Eva, the chirpy and exquisitely exuberant young woman who answered the phone, was fantastic. All over the details, super responsible, and utterly caring.

"It'll be fifteen minutes, if that's okay?" she said in her singsong voice.

Sure enough, *precisely* fifteen minutes later (I *am* in Switzerland), Eva was at my door. With a smile the size of the sun along with eyes that sparkled like a star. And a vibe that made me increase my love for being a part of the human race.

As I looked at the tray that had gently been placed upon the table in front of me, I noticed that Eva had not only put a bundle of fresh mint leaves into the teapot, she'd added a flourish: a single green artistically placed mint leaf in the ivory white teacup.

You might say, "Robin, that's such a small thing." Nope. To me, it was *gigantic*.

In an era in which so few underpromise and overdeliver, and when so many individuals want the rewards of their richest life without having to invest the commitment and do the work that a supremely rewarding life requires, Eva shone in her craft. She exemplified this fourth form of wealth. She exercised her creativity and then modeled the currency of mastery to pick off that one mint leaf and position it ever so perfectly in the teacup to make a little piece of art.

So now, I have a new metaphor for going the extra mile at work in order to mesmerize all those you meet: Maximizing the Mint Leaf. And if the habit worked for Eva, I am certain it'll work for you.

83

Be Patient Like a Pro

I'll tell you a secret to owning your game that isn't really a secret. But I'll call it a secret in the hope it'll help you pay more attention to it.

The secret is . . . *patience*.

So simple. Practical. Blindingly obvious. It's a strategy that hides in plain sight. Therefore, so few (and I do mean few) practice it with any form of consistency. "Rivers know this: there is no hurry. We shall get there some day," wrote the children's author A. A. Milne.

Today, I'm in the stylish city of Milan. The blossoms are on the trees and the flowers are on tall parade. My Italian friends and Milanese readers will hate me for telling you this, but I visited the grand Starbucks here for the first time. (I'll whisper this: it was very good.)

I listened to an amazing street musician play a Coldplay song, then something by Drake, then "Love Yourself" by Justin Bieber. (I'll whisper this, but I really like that song.)

Then I walked to the famed monument called the Duomo. Spellbinding. Breathtaking, actually.

I saw the spires and arches and the intensely intricate craftwork.

Did you know that construction began in 1386 and the final details were finished in 1965? That's *six hundred years*. On a single project.

Now let me ask you, in my most cheerful way: Do *you* have the devotion to stay with the perfecting of your Project X for *six hundred years*? Until the project is done. To sublime completion. The way it's meant to be done. In celebration of your natural talents. Makes me think of what Michelangelo said: "Genius is eternal patience."

We inhabit a civilization where most people have the attention span of a sparrow. Do you want to seriously win at work and be so far ahead of your peers that they'll never catch up to you (in *six hundred years*)?

Yes? Great.

Then become the most enduring person in your field and the most tireless producer in your arena. Sweat the most infinitesimal of details. Reach for the standards of the superstars. Don't let go. Never give up. Get the tiniest brushstrokes to grandmaster level. Then make it even better. I dare you.

84

Be Like a Dog with a Bone

Yes. Be like a dog with a bone, who doesn't let go. You see, one of the main keys to mastery is persistency. And it really is remarkable how far you can get in hot pursuit of your personal Mount Everests if you simply, absolutely and totally refuse to quit.

So straightforward. So few do this. Allow me to offer you one of my favorite examples.

Jimmy Iovine, now a titan of the music industry and a legendary record producer, wanted to woo Trent Reznor of Nine Inch Nails fame away from a small independent record company that held the rights to his music. The owner of that outfit was tough—and not at all interested in letting his prized artist leave.

Iovine's solution—as shared in the wonderful documentary *The Defiant Ones*—was to rise early every morning and perform a ritual. He'd walk into his bathroom, where he kept a phone, shut the door and call the owner. He did this each morning—at 6 AM—*for nearly an entire year*.

Eventually, the owner relented—because Jimmy Iovine was unstoppable. He admitted that he felt the producer made him feel understood and respected. So he did the deal and gave up the rights, leading to a hugely successful partnership.

In the documentary, when Iovine was asked why he wouldn't give up on acquiring Reznor for his roster of musical artists and why he called in the morning for close to 365 days in a row, he said that it's important not to let your ego get in the way of the result you're committed to achieving.

I've never forgotten that lesson. Not letting pride and looking silly in the eyes of others get in the way of realizing your target. I hope—truly—that you won't forget this instruction.

And if others do laugh at you because of your relentless belief in yourself and your ethical ambition to get a brave dream done, recall what Dr. Seuss once wrote: "Be who you are and say what you feel because those who mind don't matter and those who matter don't mind."

85

Enjoy The Time You Waste

"Time you enjoy wasting is not wasted time," noted musical maestro John Lennon.

Took me much of my early adult life to understand this one.

If I wasn't working or running my schedule or crossing off my To Do List, I felt guilty. As well as some sense of shame, I guess. Just being honest.

I see a lot of offline gurus and online influencers advising their followers to "hustle and grind" and to "use every waking moment to be productive and get ahead." Yikes!

Isn't that kind of advice merely a belief system taught to us by a culture obsessed with doing, achieving, striving, and winning? But why must winning be solely defined by getting more accomplished than others and reaching the summit of worldly success? Why are fame and fortune more prized than inner peace and personal freedom?

Why is the entrepreneur who gets a trillion things done and the billionaire who banks a ton of cash more valued (in our oh-so-strange culture) than the monk who sits in meditation in a monastery all day? Or the joyful gardener raising their bright yellow tulips?

How come the person who does their work well, then reserves their evenings for their family, passions, and human enthusiasms, is considered less "productive" than the one who is on call 24/7/365? Who sold us this bill of goods on what productivity means? And why, if we don't fill every waking hour with work, are we unworthy of being considered successful?

To go even further, why is doing nothing seen as a bad thing? Tell me. Seriously. Who sold us the idea that doing something is better than doing nothing? In truth—and I'm not sure if I'm making sense to you here—they are just different things. One really isn't better than the other, is it? Only our judgment and belief system make it so.

It's just that we've been taught by those we trust (and those who influence us) that one is better than the other.

I've learned to get really efficient at non-doing. Because a strong work ethic without a deep rest ethic won't stand the test of time.

When I work, I work swiftly, intensely, and precisely—extremely focused on the few things that count. (Confucius said it magnificently: "The person who chases two rabbits catches neither.") And when I don't work, I enjoy my life, savoring the fruits of my labor. Staring at trees as I walk in my olive grove. Taking winding drives in the countryside with Elle, making dinner for my daughter, visiting an art gallery with my son. Reading interesting books, riding my trusty mountain bike, writing in my journal, listening to country music, going for a swim in the sea.

My enthusiastic encouragement is that you become a masterful loafer at times. A total champion of doing zero when it's time to renew. Like I did last night. Just sitting outside on a cool night with a blanket over my legs, staring up at the stars. Doing nothing was really something.

86

Apply The 60-Second Anti-Procrastination Rule

Let's shift gears from the last chapter. All peak achievers have one behavior in common: they don't just dream great dreams, they also do everything necessary to get them done.

They get that ideation without execution honestly is delusion. And that the smallest of actions truly is always so much better than the grandest of intentions. In this way of operating, they show their craft that they are committed and their mastery that they are serious.

So my encouragement for you is this: *Never leave the site of a spectacular idea without doing something—anything—to bring it into reality.*

Keep repeating this mantra, over and over: "I will do it now." What you speak about shapes what you'll produce in the world. And then, when a bold and audacious inspiration surfaces, take swift action—within sixty seconds—to make even the smallest bit of progress on it. So that you defeat procrastination. And always keep moving forward.

"Until one is committed, there is hesitancy, the chance to draw back, always ineffectiveness. Concerning all acts of initiative and creation, there is one elementary truth, the ignorance of which kills countless ideas and splendid plans: that the moment one definitely commits oneself, then providence moves too," said mountaineer William Hutchison Murray.

I guess he was teaching us that there's a difference between busyness and productivity, movement and progress.

And that nothing happens until we start.

87

While You're Working, Keep Improving

I recently overheard a conversation I need to tell you about.

I was having lunch in a restaurant. A man wanted a glass of red wine. He pointed to a variety on the menu. The server looked at the wine list and then said, "This one? I'm not going to pronounce the name properly, but I'll try."

He then mangled the name of the wine. And walked off to get it for the guest.

Just out of curiosity, when the server came to our table, I asked him how long he'd worked at the restaurant.

"This will be my eleventh year," he replied proudly.

Hmmm . . . Eleven years. At this restaurant. Taking orders for food and wine. Spending many of his most valuable hours here. Giving his incredibly precious life energy to this job. Given the opportunity to be an expert at what he does. To become a merchant of wow. To receive huge tips.

Yet for some reason, he didn't seem to take his work—his craft (a currency that could bring him not only vast professional, financial and personal rewards but spiritual ones too)—seriously. He never took the time to study the wine list so he could learn to pronounce the names properly. It appeared to me he just showed up, day after day. For eleven years.

As a contrast, consider Ferran Adrià, the founder and chef of the iconic Michelin three-star restaurant El Bulli. Known for leading the field of molecular gastronomy, providing his guests thirty-four-course meals, and mesmerizing fellow chefs by his monomaniacal obsession with getting details flawless, at the height of El Bulli's fame (two million people applied each season to get one of the rare reservations), Adrià closed the place.

Although he could have made a financial fortune with his creations (his "chicken curry" turned the traditional recipe on its head by placing the chicken sauce over curry ice cream) and he was heralded as "the best cook on the planet" by super-chef Joël Robuchon, he shuttered his shop because he felt he had gone as far as he could as a chef. And needed to explore fresh challenges for his growth as an artist.

Here's the takeaway: the moment you're at the top of your game and near the apex of your powers is the minute you need to push yourself to shatter your winning formula, recalibrate the skills that have served you so well, and imagine new ways to completely reinvent yourself. The alternative? Mediocrity. And a quick descent into obscurity.

88

Labor for The Magic, Never for The Money

Superstar athlete and supreme entrepreneur Shaquille O'Neal was on my faculty for a live event and shared three powerful lessons I trust will bring value to you. I'll jump right into them:

Lesson #1: Keep Your Kids Humble and Grounded. When his children would say, "Dad, let's buy this—we're rich," he'd reply, "You're not rich, I am." The old adage "shirtsleeves to shirtsleeves in three generations" is generally true. Financial wealth is often made by the first, enjoyed by the second and lost in the third.

Lesson #2: Remember Your Roots. Too many people reach world-class success in their field then forget who brought them to the dance. Shaq explained to my audience that before every home game the Lakers would play, he'd drive to his former neighborhood—in a poor area of Los Angeles—and shoot hoops with the kids on the street. Then he'd get back into his car and drive to the game. I asked him why he would do this. His reply was classic: "Because those kids used to be me."

Lesson #3: Never Work Purely for the Money. Shaq shared that—as an entrepreneur—when he did a deal only for the promise of a massive cash jackpot, the ventures always failed. Yet when he accepted an opportunity because it inspired him, because it would force him to grow as a leader and because it just felt right, the results were inevitably excellent.

Yes, my friend, do your work for more than just the money. Do it for the growth it will give you. Do it for the talents it will introduce you to. Do it for the person it will make of you. Do it for the meaning it will deliver to you. And of course—always—do your work supremely well (with positivity and passion even if no one's watching) for the people you will help, and the better world you'll build.

89

The Michelin-Three-Star with The Very Absent Chef

At my leadership keynotes, I say to my audiences: "Nothing fails like success." When you're most successful is the very point when you're most vulnerable. When you're winning you're just a few missteps away from losing. Success is super dangerous! Once there, you think because you're at the top of your craft, you'll always remain at the top. You stop innovating and are more open to coasting. You take your customers for granted and your lasting dominance as a given. At such a time, it's ever so easy to slip into the near-invisible decline that eventually leads to defeat.

To avoid this, you must stay deeply hungry. And remarkably scrappy. Always ready to learn new things, take fresh risks, deliver the unexpected, fail on the way to innovation, become even more grateful for the food on your family's table, and operate from a white-belt mentality.

Last autumn, I took my son on a trip to the north of Italy. I'd recently done a father-daughter adventure, so it was Colby's turn. We went on a truffle hunt with a dog named Lady, took long walks in the mountains, and did a cooking lesson (we made ravioli).

On one evening—as a special treat for our last night—I booked a reservation at a three-star Michelin restaurant. I'd been there before with Elle and the food was exceptionally great (especially the poached eggs with pecorino cheese, fresh cream and white truffles).

So we showed up ready to be blown away. To experience one of the great meals of our lives. A father and his son.

Guess what? The chef was there, but not in the kitchen this time. Instead, she was at a large table next to us, the one by the roaring fire. She was with about six of her friends. Talking. Laughing. Drinking expensive red wine. Telling stories of her glory days. She still had her white chef's uniform on, although she did no cooking that night.

I don't know about you, but if I'm going to splurge on a special occasion and go to a Michelin three-star restaurant (which I've done only twice in my life), I want the chef who received the three Michelin stars to make my food.

And the food? Mediocre. Truly. Just okay. Nothing special. One course was almost inedible. So I've been to that place two times: the first time and the last time.

What's my point with this mild rant? Easy. The chef became a top chef at a top restaurant. Then she took her winning for granted and rested on her laurels. Lost her fire. Thought no one would notice. Stopped making sure every ingredient was exquisite and each meal was perfect.

As you continue to reach new levels of mastery, remember this story. And never take your victory for granted. Because nothing fails like success. And if you forget this rule, you'll get knocked out of the game sooner than you could imagine.

90

Life Is More Important Than Work

Kenny Sailors is my current hero. Because he reminded me that, while doing your best work is a central element of a truly rich life, it's far from everything that one needs to live beautifully.

The other night, I stayed up late to watch the furiously inspiring documentary *Jump Shot*.

It was about, well, the jump shot.

And how this now-common basketball move was invented, how it shook the sport, and how it spread through the generations.

Yet what I saw was about so much more.

The documentary suggested that, as a young man, Kenny Sailors was the one who created the jump shot. This was at a time, the 1940s, when—as odd as it seems—basketball players kept their feet on the ground as they took their shots. Getting airtime was an utterly radical notion.

What Kenny did had never been dared. It was less a stroke of innovation than an act of revolution, for the sport.

Fans were stunned. Players were awestruck. Basketball was changed. *Forever.*

Kenny Sailors became the Kobe, the Jordan, the LeBron of his age. Dominant. Celebrated. Revered. Adored.

And then, he *vanished*.

He went to World War II. Fought as a Marine. Risked his life. For his country.

On his return, he and his cherished wife moved to the woods of remote Alaska. There, he hunted, fished, and built camps. Lived off the land. Raised a family. Rode horses. Played zero basketball. Instead, Kenny made a life.

The couple led this austere existence for thirty-five years, until his wife began to suffer from dementia. Which broke his heart.

After her passing, he lived quietly. He began to mentor young basketball players and served his community, often anonymously. (The finest way to give, right?)

Near the end of his life, Kenny Sailors was asked about his "Final Four"—a term used for the important playoff matches in college basketball, where all teams in the league have been eliminated except for the finest four. The interviewer was now spinning the term into a question that was really about the four most important things to him.

"God, being a great husband, a loving father and a good Marine."

Basketball wasn't even on the list.

Kenny died at ninety-five. As a hero. In my eyes—and in the eyes of many.

This humble man lived simply, honorably, happily, and with deep integrity. The real takeaway of this mentoring message? When it comes to pursuing your craft and rising to absolutely world-class as you perform it, do it with all the genius, strength and enthusiasm you have within you. And when you're not working, lead a quiet, thoughtful, honorable, and meaningful life. Because making a great living must never prevent you from constructing a gorgeous life.

THE 5TH FORM OF WEALTH

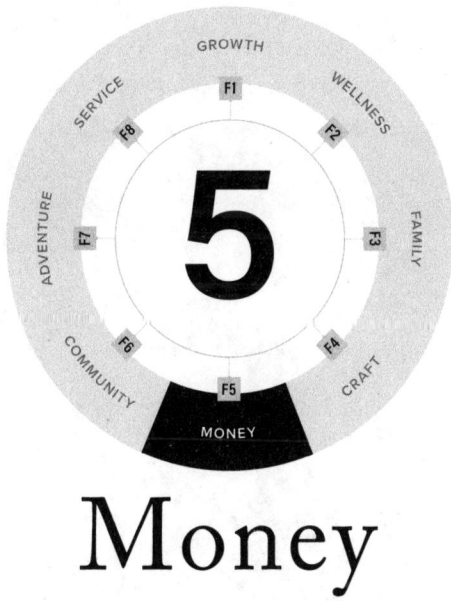

Money

The Prosperity as Fuel for Freedom Habit

*If we command our wealth, we shall be rich and free;
if our wealth commands us, we are poor indeed.*
—Edmund Burke

The 5th Form of Wealth
Money | Quick Overview

Having enough income and financial worth to have the sense that you can live life on your own terms (and with the freedom to lead the lifestyle that you want for yourself and your loved ones) is not only an important element of a *truly* rich life, but an essential one.

The key is to use money to serve you rather than becoming a captive to the pursuit of cash, allowing all seven of the other currencies of wealth to be neglected. You never, ever want to be financially rich and happiness poor, right?

This makes me think of a fascinating story that appeared in an issue of *The New Yorker*. Famed authors Joseph Heller and Kurt Vonnegut were at a cocktail party at the home of a Wall Street titan on Long Island. It was glamorous, filled with socialites and glittered with excess.

Vonnegut asked his friend, "Joe, how does it feel to know that our host made more money yesterday than you'll make from all your royalties for *Catch-22*?"

Heller replied, "Well, Kurt, I have something he'll never have."

"What's that?" his friend inquired.

"The feeling of enough," was the simple response.

The feeling of enough. Beautiful. To know the fulfillment of being satisfied with what you have makes you wealthy. Having said this, encouraging yourself to acquire reasonable financial riches *is* necessary to live your finest life. Economic prosperity allows you the liberty to make the choices that are in your best interests rather than being forced into a corner, having to do things you don't want to do but have to do because you need the paycheck. Money abundance also provides you and your loved ones with easier circumstances, and the opportunity to enjoy the wonderful pleasures that the material world offers.

It's really a balance, isn't it? Own your cash rather than letting it own you. Let a sensible amount of affluence serve you so you experience a marvelous lifestyle. Yet never allow money to become your master. Ever.

With this context, let us begin our journey through the lessons I have carefully prepared for you to significantly increase the fifth of the eight forms of wealth—money—in your valuable life. Shall we begin?

91

Avoid The Howard Hughes Money Trap

Last night, I watched an alternately inspiring and shocking documentary on Howard Hughes, a man who—in his era—was one of the planet's richest people. It struck me as a good place to begin our discussion of the fifth form of wealth. "Why?" you wonder. Allow me to explain.

> ... He made fifty million dollars a year (equivalent to one hundred and fifty million now) from his tool company.
> ... He sold TWA stock (from his airline) for half a billion in cash (back in 1966).
> ... He pioneered new planes as a master aviator and launched an innovative Hollywood studio.
> ... He even invented the automatic hospital bed after being frustrated by having to lie flat constantly after suffering severe injuries in a plane crash.

Here's the thing, though. While he was super rich, his later years were spent alone, in a near-always-dark penthouse of a hotel in Las Vegas. No family around him, struggling with drug addiction and poor health, suffering from the lack of any real enjoyment of the gift that is a human life.

Hughes was so powerful, so unreachable in a way, that he was isolated from anyone who could have spoken truth to him—and helped him reconnect with reality. Top managers around him shielded the mogul from the serious challenges that were unfolding within his empire. And his personal demons ensured that while he had all the money in the world he lived as a hermit locked in his lavish yet filthy hotel suite.

As the complexity of his operations grew, he attracted people who didn't always have his best interests in mind, and failed to ensure that he got appropriate treatment for his mental health struggles. As things declined, he spent his days naked—refusing to bathe, terrified of germs, and frightened of other people. He was left in the shadows, with needles in his arms for long stretches of time. A very sad ending to an exceptional man's life.

Let's be clear: the making of money is not an evil pursuit. Money really can make your lifestyle so much easier and solve many problems. Money can allow you to do so much good for your family and enrich your community. Many of the famous (but quiet) billionaires I've advised over all these decades are some of the most high-integrity, generous, and kind people I've met, sincerely working to be sure that they are making the world significantly better.

I guess what I'm really suggesting to you—my steadily growing friend—is simply that as you increase your financial wealth, please be careful to make certain it becomes a gateway into goodness instead of a prison that destroys your happiness.

92

Know Your Scarcity Scars

Making money to grow the fifth form of wealth is not an accident. Instead, the accumulation of financial prosperity happens through the conscious and consistent application of a set of time-tested rules that those who have money know, use, and optimize.

A wise starting point to upgrade your economic abundance is to heal your money wounds. These are the false beliefs and emotional injuries that have been formed as you've advanced through your life. Especially in our youth, we adopt the thinking of our parents and early teachers on money (remember the five forces of PENAM that I walked you through much earlier in our time together?). And as we grow older, we experience disappointments, trials, and losses in this area that close us to possibilities, limit us from welcoming opportunity, and cause us to become cynical about our potential to be a financial force on the planet (or at least to be free of daily money stresses).

Perhaps you have been taught by those you trust that "rich people are thieves," that "the wealthy are different from us," that "money is the root of all evil" or that "those with plenty of funds just got lucky." Or maybe you were told that "investing in the stock market is gambling" (it only is if you don't know how to assess the value of a company and so take shots in the dark) or that "buying foreign real estate is foolish" (it only is if your purchase is an uninformed one). If you have these beliefs, do you really think you'll have the ambition to learn and then apply the rules that will bring your highest money potential to life? The core beliefs you hold very much do become self-fulfilling prophecies. *Human beings get what they expect.*

Today, I strongly encourage you to start the process of healing your financial wealth wounds. So you fully get to enjoy all of the benefits this type of currency brings. Here are four proven practices to help you wire in the mentality of prosperity and the emotionality of a healthier relationship with your income:

1. Treat Yourself Like Visiting Royalty. I'm in no way suggesting that you go out and purchase something you cannot afford. I'm a huge fan of being frugal. Yet I am sure there are some actions you could take *immediately* to celebrate all you've become and to reward yourself for all you've overcome.

Ideas include having a simple ceremony where you find a quiet, beautiful place to honor all the skills you've developed and all the value you've created for others (recall that money is the by-product of value delivered to your marketplace), or having a massage at a top spa, or taking the trip you've always longed to take, or investing in a piece of original art from an unknown yet superb local artist that you joyfully hang in your home. I'm inviting you to do something—anything—to appreciate yourself for all you've grown into because this will increase what I call in my mentoring work DeserveAbility. Here's the principle: *As you treat yourself better, you'll naturally feel you deserve better.* This, in turn, will cause you to seize more excellent opportunities, push better work into your field, and raise the fees you ask clients to pay (and fire the ones who steal your joy).

As you continue to elevate your personal appreciation, you'll raise your standards around the quality of your daily habits, your physical fitness, the amounts you ask for in negotiations, the goodness of the content you consume, the caliber of your friendships, and the specialness of the places you go to. Yes, increasing your self-worth leads to an inevitable rise in your net worth. *Money doesn't like people who don't love themselves.*

2. Visit Super-Rich Places. The next principle here can be stated easily: Prosperity is an energy, so be around its vitality.

You have to do this carefully, yet being around luxury will increase and then normalize your confidence to build more prosperity in your life. Deep within, you'll know you just belong in such high-end places. And soon you'll automatically start creating the mastery that will make this lifestyle real. *Income always reflects identity* (read that twice).

This might initially simply look like enjoying a cup of tea at the café of an ultra-chic department store or having a salad at the restaurant of the most exquisite hotel in your city. By placing yourself in such environments, you'll hear the conversations of people with prosperity. You'll be in a position to make new connections. And your perception of yourself along with your honoring of your talents will subtly and progressively begin to shift. Trust me on this, please. Money really is a strong reflection of the way you see yourself. As you start to view yourself as a much more prosperous person, you'll begin doing the things prosperous people do. Which will certainly make you more money.

3. Do a Scarcity Inventory. In your morning journal, list all the mind programs your parents, your teachers, and the media have taught you about the negativity of making, cultivating, and protecting money. Also record your wealth wounds: those hurts that happened when you tried to grow your prosperity and it didn't work out. Writing all this down will bring the causes that have limited your economic progress into sharper focus and out into the open

where you can see how they have been sabotaging your winning in this fifth form of wealth. Shadows brought into the light dissolve and awareness precedes transformation. As Maya Angelou advised, "Do the best you can until you know better. Then, when you know better, do better."

4. Create Your Ideal Life Collage. You know I'm very much an evangelist for execution. No idea works for someone unwilling to do any work. And excellent things unfold for people who do excellent things. Having said this, clarity breeds mastery and you need to do the up-front thinking to know what you want before you take the action to bring it to life. How can you get what you desire if you have no clue what you need? Vague plans lead to vague performance. Definitely don't invest your best years climbing mountains that, at the end, turn out to be the wrong ones.

So start the process of reprogramming, upgrading and then electrifying your mind to focus purely on the rich lifestyle you seek. One superb tool to do this is a dream collage on a large board that you will see daily. This collage contains pictures of the majestic life you'll experience once you have made the financial wealth to enjoy it. The images may be of a home that you'd like to live in with your loved ones, tropical islands or ski resorts where you hope to vacation, cars you wish to own, clothes you want to wear, top restaurants you aspire to visit, super-fun adventures you'd like to take, and charities you're set to serve. Again, the key here is to enjoy material things (because we do live in a material world), yet never to *need* the things you own. And to avoid defining yourself by your possessions.

Okay. It's autumn at the old farmhouse and the colors are pretty breathtaking. If you were here with me—maybe having a cup of fresh mint tea—I think you'd agree. Although I don't ride my mountain bike like a wild man, as I used to when I was younger, I'll hit the trails now. For a gentle spin. Let's talk later. Bye.

93

Your Vitality Serves You Financially

Just about every one of the money masters I've been around is extremely fit. They work out most mornings, walk a lot (and adore walking meetings), invest in the best exercise machines, and have personal trainers, massage therapists, and nutritionists. They profoundly understand that one of the great keys to legendary prosperity is developing limitless energy.

Many of the ones I've mentored meditate, monitor the quality of their sleep to optimize it, take ice baths, sweat daily in hot saunas, breathe fresh air regularly, and go to longevity clinics to, well, extend their longevity. (Pro tip: if you're seriously serious about living your richest life, *don't die*.)

You might wonder when they find the time to work. Well, such souls are usually minimalists: they say no to most activities so they can get to the highest level on only a few. They are essentialists versus maximalists, if you get my drift.

Even more importantly, they profoundly understand that money invested in arriving at their finest health and peak vitality is absolutely necessary for their financial mastery. They get that mission number one to reach the summit of economic prosperity is not to get sick. Sure, all the things they do that I've listed cost money. But disease costs you more.

More healthy equals more energy. More energy means greater productivity. More productivity results in superior value sent out into your industry. And the natural reply of the marketplace to humans who create splendid products and services that make the lives of others better is higher income. If you and I were sitting together in person in my library in front of a roaring fire, I'd draw a model from my mentoring methodology on another napkin that would sort of look like this:

BETTER HEALTH = MORE ENERGY: ▲ GREATER PRODUCTIVITY = DEEPER VALUE TO YOUR INDUSTRY ▶ HIGHER INCOME

Yes, elevating your health raises the vitality that drives your productivity and that boosts value delivery into the economy, which results in you enjoying greater prosperity.

Oh, and if you lengthen your lifespan by ten or twenty years by installing the correct habits of health, just think about how many more people you will enrich. Which makes me think about how much more money you'll make as a result of this extended helpfulness. As I once heard iconic billionaire Ted Turner say, "He profits most who serves best." Wisdom.

94

The Top Move of Money Masters

One of the prime habits for success in the fifth form of wealth, after increasing your health and energy, is to think for yourself. This is a main driver of the victory experienced by financial empire-makers.

These people don't mind being ridiculed for the sake of remaining true to their instincts, intuitions, and brave vision for a better future. Actually, they take the stones their critics throw at them and make them into movements that stand as testimony to their audacity.

Our current culture is one where the majority of us follow the crowd, model ourselves on what influencers do (and buy, eat and say), and operate as we are told to operate. Too many among us are becoming more obedient "sheeple" versus stronger and wiser people.

Last week I read a review of a book on creativity written by a star music producer. The critic was highly attacking of the work, because that's what critics do (if they had the talent and guts to do the work they are condemning, they would have done it!).

... He said that the book wasn't much of a memoir (yet it wasn't meant to be a memoir).

... He wrote that the book didn't share many anecdotes of the producer's experiences in the studio with the musical superstars he worked with (it wasn't meant to be about that; it's a sharing of his insights on the creative process).

... He noted that the book didn't deliver much value and suggested it wasn't worth buying.

After reviewing the review, I looked at the online comments.

"Thanks for the helpful review. You saved me from having to buy this book," said one.

Hmmm. I have heard only good things about the impact of this übercreative man, who is more of an artist than a producer. And because I'm beyond fascinated by how artists upgrade their game and make work that mesmerizes others, I quickly purchased the audiobook, regardless of the negativity surrounding it.

Guess what? It's one of the finest, most helpful, and truly thoughtful guides for leveraging human creativity and releasing masterwork that I have ever read.

The lesson for us is this: *Think for yourself.*

I honestly doubt that the critic even read the book from beginning to end. Seriously. (By the way, that reminds me of yet another thing that billionaires do: they go deep rather than wide, and granular on anything they decide to win at, instead of superficial and light.)

And I'm fairly sure the critic is not a serious creative, because I don't think he understood what the author was saying. It makes me remember what Bob Dylan once advised: "Don't criticize what you can't understand."

Your takeaway from this chapter: because those who commented took what they read in the review as gospel (without thinking for themselves), they missed out on learning ideas and tools that would have helped them maximize their artistry, exponentially.

One even said, "You don't need a book to learn how to express your creativity. You just need to do it."

Really? How silly.

As if the hard-earned wisdom written by a human being who has been working the craft for decades—at the highest grade on the planet—cannot be helpful to avoid mistakes, shorten the expertise curve, and provoke one's imagination to accomplish things that were previously viewed as impossible.

Trust your own opinions. And fortify your faith for your exciting mission, along with protecting your honest inclinations—even if the entire tribe is laughing at you. Every visionary is initially ridiculed, before they are revered.

95

The Multibillionaire in The Very Empty Mansion

A few years ago, my team received a request from a celebrated entrepreneurial icon. He wanted me to help him add another zero or two to his fortune while getting his health back to good and finding more joy, peace, and freedom in his ridiculously complicated life.

After deeply considering the request for a few weeks, I agreed to meet the tycoon. I flew many hours to his home city in a distant country, checked into my hotel, and reviewed my preparation notes so I would be on my game when I met him. (Another pro tip: always be the most prepared person in every room you're in—because if you're not overprepared you're not prepared.)

I hopped into a cab, which led me past famous buildings, along tree-lined boulevards and up to an area that appeared to be populated with embassies, sprawling estates, and gargantuan mansions.

The taxi pulled up to one of the largest, grandest, and most sensational homes I've ever seen. An aide met me at the soaring wrought-iron gates and walked me past fragrant flower gardens, elaborate outdoor sculptures by renowned artists, and a series of architecturally stunning guest cottages.

Eventually, we arrived at the main house in the primary area of the expansive compound. The assistant opened the front door, walked me through the marble foyer and through a living room where clearly priceless paintings hung on the walls, fabulous oriental rugs covered the floors, and custom-designed furniture held stacks and stacks of business books.

We traveled along a long hallway, down a set of stairs and into what appeared to be an underground complex.

A glass wall revealed a garage filled with Ferraris and Lamborghinis and Bugattis. To the left was another hallway that led us to a metal door. I could smell cigar smoke.

"He's inside waiting for you, Mr. Sharma," said the right hand. "He's in a good mood today so you will enjoy your meeting very much. He's really been looking forward to seeing you."

The door opened, revealing a huge office with a wide reclaimed-wood table in the center, with neat piles of paper organized across it. Floor-to-ceiling shelves held yet more books. "For Whom the Bell Tolls" by Metallica was playing. Yes, Metallica was playing.

A long cigar puff. Smoke filled the space.

The client was in his early 40s and sported a black hoodie, black sweatpants, and a black baseball cap over his wavy brown hair. On one wrist was a big stainless steel watch and on the other was a series of thin red strings. Though he was relatively young, he looked old. Weary. And very much out of shape.

The renowned billionaire and I chatted for more than three hours. I asked a ton of questions and took pages and pages of notes. I inquired about his current life, his largest triumphs, and his deepest sufferings. I examined his hopes and dreams. I probed him on his entertainment empire and his various investments. I gently questioned him on his morning routine, work rituals, pre-sleep structure, and overall lifestyle.

Then I said, "Please tell me about your family." My research hadn't been able to reveal much about the magnate's personal life and my guess is that his business team had been instructed to scrub the internet of all details. For whatever reason.

A long pause. Another long puff on the cigar.

"No one."

"What do you mean?" I replied. "You must have some people you care about and people who care about you. You don't live here at this complex alone, do you?"

"Yep," was the straightforward reply. "It's just me here. And my team of assistants. No family. No real friends. Pretty much alone."

He looked away. I heard a sigh.

I won't reveal anything further of this meeting. And I share it only to reinforce a cautionary tale: Many with a lot of money are actually stuck in poverty. There are many incredibly important things that money—which, after all is only *one* form of the eight forms of wealth—can't buy. Having enough is certainly important and that's why I'm walking you through this section. But in an age when society generally measures worldly success solely by the size of someone's bank account and the wealth in their stock portfolio, I'm humbly and gently reminding you that there's no point in devoting your life to scaling this seemingly satisfying summit only to reach the top completely alone. And fully empty.

96

Grateful Is a Money Printer

It's a sunny day on the farm. I see vineyards in the distance, hear dogs barking and am uplifted by the birdsong that I hear through the window of my writing room. Not sure why but in this era of so much complexity, birds singing make me happy.

All right. Let's get into this next lesson with this idea: you'll see more of what you focus on in your life. What you pay attention to is an amplifier and what you center your mind upon is a maximizer. So don't keep ruminating about what's not working when you have the choice to obsess on what's great today.

Which brings us even deeper into the importance of gratefulness. Gratitude is the antidote to fear, you know. And a gateway practice into prosperity.

When you're wallowing in scarcity and restricted by insecurity because you're worried about things and catastrophizing over your future, you miss opportunities, degrade your productivity, and fail to incubate the ideas that could make you your fortune. From a metaphysical viewpoint, not giving thanks for the gifts you have tells the universe you're not appreciative for all the blessings in your life, which blocks the flow of more.

What you appreciate appreciates in value and what you celebrate escalates your delight.

So—as simple as it sounds—while Pink's uplifting tune "Cover Me in Sunshine" plays in my messy writing room (with my faithful dog next to me), I suggest you count your gifts. Turn (and train) your perception to those things that increase your joy and make you feel safe, good, and successful. The energy of this positivity will allow more money to flood into your life. Yes, it most certainly will.

97

See Another's Winning as Your Victory

Financial freedom is rarely found by jealous people. There, I said it.

Jealousy is a thought (and heart) poison that ruins your creativity, pollutes your productivity, minimizes your bravery, and keeps you from growing into the highest version of your finest vision.

The time you spend feeling animosity for someone else's victories steals time you might have spent producing your own. It's just a completely unuseful habit. And one that is unworthy of your rich, great and noble character.

"So, Robin, how do I stop being jealous of the good fortune of others?" you may courageously ask.

"Just stop," I'd gently yet firmly say.

- ... Stop scrolling to see what others are doing and what they are accomplishing.
- ... Stop comparing yourself to influencers and stand up for your own your uniqueness, giftedness, and specialness. There are talents *you* have that the people you admire only dream of having.

... Stop wanting what you see another possessing because maybe the wisdom that rules the world knows something you don't and has decided that what you want isn't best for you.

I guess what I'm really trying to tell you—with a ton of love and respect—is what's right for you is coming to you and what's not yours won't be yours. So why would you want it?

And, even more importantly, start practicing the fantastic habit of feeling happy at the sign of someone else's accomplishment, triumph, and winning. With focus and steady effort (we get better at what we practice, right?), within only a few weeks you'll make good gains in reprogramming and restructuring your inner architecture to become a nonjealous person, who operates in a way that causes great experiences to come your way too.

Last thought to consider here: If someone's jealous of you, it's because they think you're better than them. And have the life they secretly want.

98

Remember The Habits Beat IQ Slogan

Top habits are more valuable to financial riches than off-the-chart intelligence, every day of the week. Memorize that brain tattoo, sing it in the streets and then shout that slogan from the rooftops. Because it's *incredibly* important.

Actually—and I'm going out on a limb here—many of the multibillionaires I've mentored are not the smartest people on the planet. They are bright, for sure, but not more than the average person. In my experience, being *too* smart and *too* academic and *too* well-educated causes one to overthink things. And to accept only what the status quo says is reasonable. Yet all inventions, innovations, and advancements came from a creator who thought (and then did) the impossible.

Remember Roger Bannister, the runner? Everyone said no human being could run a mile in under four minutes. And if they did, it was believed, their body would explode. The runner would likely die. But Bannister was a possibilitarian. So he did his daily training, ate properly, rested well, studied his sport, remained positive and then ran his best race, breaking the barrier. Interestingly, within weeks of his showing what was possible, others started running the mile in under four minutes.

Makes me recall one of my favorite quotes, from the Irish playwright George Bernard Shaw: "The reasonable man adapts himself to the world; the unreasonable one persists in trying to adapt the world to himself. Therefore, all progress depends on the unreasonable man."

Anyway, my main point is that the great men and women who have created rich financial fortunes are not those with the highest IQs but the finest habits.

Install excellent ones into your days. And spend some time now reflecting on this rule that the most precise way to improve your money future is to enrich the routines you're running today.

99
—
Use Wealth Words

I'd like to say more on the power of the words you use, in this mentoring session together.

The words we speak carry such influence and have such energy. Too many good souls among us are too loose with their vocabulary. And trust me, this seriously reduces their prosperity.

In my leadership presentations, I always talk about the supreme power of words. I start by reminding my audience to strip gossip out of their communications and to completely avoid saying bad things about other people as, at some level, they can sense it. As well, when you speak poorly about others, be certain they'll be speaking poorly about you.

Then I say to my audiences, "Use leadertalk versus victimspeak." Deploy weak words and not only will your performance be reduced, you'll push all those around you—who could help you accomplish your mighty mission and ethical ambitions—away from you because no one is attracted to negativity, apathy, and toxicity.

As always, the beginning of transformation is to increase your awareness around the quality of your language. As you become clearer on the low-quality words you send out into the universe, you can begin to make those all-important micro-improvements to raise your communication skills to the next level of mastery. Small, daily, seemingly insignificant optimizations—when done consistently over time—really do lead to *stunning* results!

To be practical, I offer you this list of words to use daily to boost your influence, performance, and economic prosperity:

Possible	Leadership	Sensational
Can	Focus	Wonderful
Mastery	Helpful	Astonishing
Yes	Excellence	Positive
Brave	Grateful	Heroic
Powerful	Creativity	Grow
Consistency	Magic	Inspired
Opportunity	Limitless	Generous
Beautiful	Willpower	Wisdom
Improvement	Love	Committed
Transform	Genius	Service

Autosuggestion truly is an easy, strong, and super-practical tool to own more of your native power and to become a more honest and influential leader, communicator, and human being who builds the currency that will generate more money.

100

Run The Tracey Emin Anti-Cocaine Rule

I'm a big fan of British artist Tracey Emin. Her art just speaks to me, enchants me, and sometimes confuses me. All of which simply makes me feel more alive. And more daring creatively.

In a very cool interview with the *Financial Times*, she admitted that she is good with money. She owns a complex of properties in Margate, England, a house in the South of France, and a chic townhouse at Fitzroy Square in London.

Here's the part I love best:

> As an artist, you're not supposed to admit that because being good with money means you're not creative, you're not spiritual. The reason I have been brilliant with money is that in the 1990s I never took cocaine. *Ever*. I think I saved the same amount of money to buy my first house as most people back then were putting up their noses.

Her point is a wise one for any financial wealth-maker: *Do not waste your hard-earned money.* Ever.

Don't just avoid snorting it up your nose. Don't waste this reward for your ingenuity rendered to the marketplace on:

>... expensive and constant restaurant meals that reduce your good health and cost you valuable energy
>
>... clothes you only wear once and costly watches that sit in a drawer
>
>... slick cars and sleek hotels that provide you with cool selfies to impress people yet have next to zero return on investment

I get that this is common sense yet common sense is pretty rare these days.

101

Live Beneath Your Means

Yesterday I spent an hour talking to a financial leader known in some circles as "the banker to billionaires."

A friend of a friend knows him. The banker reads my books and asked to have coffee with me.

I came prepared with questions that I believed were thoughtful. So that I too could learn from the time spent together, and so there wouldn't be any awkward silences that sometimes show up when you meet someone new.

I loved meeting him! He was gracious, humble, and interesting.

The gentleman was an excellent listener, a rich thinker, and a person who had clearly spent a lot of time calibrating his personal philosophy on the way he wanted to show up and operate in the world.

When I asked him, "What's your best financial advice?" he responded quickly: "No leverage." (Yes, I get this is contrary to the common advice that others will give you around using OPM—Other People's Money—to grow your fortune. There are many ways to build financial freedom and nothing in life is black and white, is it?)

He went on to explain that "an investor's best friend is time." Time allows money to compound over a long horizon. And as you know, compounding can cause *exponential* growth in your wealth when you have the discipline to wait and wait and wait.

"But if you have borrowed money, a time might come when the bank becomes a wolf at your door, wanting their money back. Which means you won't get the benefits of compounding. So it's smart to live below your means and invest without any leverage."

We all know we should do it, yet it's a rule that's generally practiced in the breach. I'm reminded of investment guru Warren Buffett's wisdom on the danger of too much debt: "Only when the tide goes out do you discover who's been swimming naked."

A client who founded a top hedge fund once shared a money insight that remains with me to this moment: "The real reason most people don't get ahead financially is that as they increase their income, they also increase their lifestyle costs. They make more money and then, rather than using a relatively small amount on their lifestyle and investing the rest intelligently, they use the extra money to buy into a neighborhood where wealthier people live. This then puts pressure on them to buy the cars their neighbors have, vacation on the Caribbean islands their community goes to for vacations, and send their kids to the same incredibly expensive schools the people next door send their children to. So, at the end of each year, they are still left with nothing to save and invest. Often, though they are growing in income, they end up deeper into debt."

So before you rush to make your next purchase, practice a tool that I call The 24 Hour Temptation Reducer. Sleep on the buy. Wait twenty-four hours and then see how you feel about the purchase. More often than not, the temptation will vanish. Your impulse to get what you wanted in that moment will have dissolved. And your more sensible (and responsible) thinking will have returned, saving you money (a ton over time). So many poor money decisions are made by people who were tired (or bored or angry or hungry) when they made them.

And *definitely* do ensure that you live beneath your means so you can wisely invest your money in sensible things versus the shiny toys that you'll regret owning in the future.

The entire multibillion-dollar storage business has been created because so many of us buy far more than we need. Reduce your wants—and instead simply serve your *needs*—and just watch the bounty that flows. Buying less also reduces waste on the planet so you're doing good for Mother Earth (and the happiness of future generations).

"The way to wealth depends chiefly on two words: industry and frugality; that is, waste neither time nor money, but make the best use of both." This is advice from the writer, inventor, statesman, and philosopher Benjamin Franklin (read his autobiography, by the way; it's one of the best books in my library). It's advice worth memorizing.

102
The Habit Stack of Super-Wealthy People

Super-wealthy people have the following nine habits in common, in addition to the ones I've already mentioned:

Habit #1: Monomaniacal Focus. At a time when the majority is suffering from Broken Focus Syndrome, the money moguls have *developed* the magnificent ability to concentrate almost completely on the near-flawless execution of the few projects that will make their ethical ambitions real. When they work, they do real work versus fake work and understand the uselessness of being busy being busy. And wasting hours of their finest days mindlessly browsing online or following trivial pursuits.

Habit #2: Undefeatable Positivity. Finacial titans are unbreakable optimists. They value a better world because of their innovations and hope for a richer future because of their inventions. They are masters of entrepreneurship instead of entitlement, really believing that their creativity, productivity, teamwork, and contributions to their industry are dramatically more essential to their success than having a fortunate destiny or getting lucky.

Habit #3: Unique Unorthodoxy. They really do see what we all see, yet think what few dare. They avoid the attraction to copying. Such individuals are profoundly imaginative, dreaming up extraordinary plans for new ventures that disrupt existing enterprises and deliver fresh benefits to millions of consumers. They know that unless they are being called crazy a lot they are not dreaming big enough. And they pretty much couldn't care less about the disapproval of others.

Habit #4: Extreme Resolve. They stay with their high-value targets through the storms of criticism, the attacks of vicious critics, and the aching bouts of self-doubt. Much like that dog with a bone, these movement-makers have habituated (by training) the traits of resilience and persistence and the superhuman determination to finish what they start. Billionaires have built the ability to take great pain. And keep on going *forever*.

Habit #5: Intelligent Risk-Taking. Magnates are not at all foolish when it comes to seizing opportunity and maximizing victory. Not at all. Instead, they are masters of "hedged risk-taking." They take risks that have a very high chance of turning into massive wins. A key here is to remember "no ask, no get" and "zero risk, zero reward."

Habit #6: Managed Perfectionism. Yes—these souls are mostly absolute perfectionists. If they are founders of a hotel chain they just might delay the opening of a new property for two months if the marble they ordered for the restaurant is not the precise color. If they are a tech company founder they'll insist on getting the product to Mona Lisa–level exquisiteness before it's released (Steve Jobs wanted the icons on the iPhone to be so magical users would want to lick the screen). If they are entertainment virtuosos they'll be relentless in making sure that their film or album is *astonishingly* well made, no matter how much they have to suffer to get the job done.

Habit #7: Leader Building. Great leaders build more leaders. (Read that twice, please, because if you're not growing more leaders then you're not really leading, just following.) One of the top ways financial sovereigns scale their fortunes is by exploiting *leverage*. And that's not only leveraging in terms of "good debt"; what I really mean is leverage through the honest development of leadership talent of the people around you. As you grow more leaders who can execute on your mighty mission with military-like mastery, you're freed up to do *only* what you do best (and love most). You just can't do it alone. And the greater your dream, the more important it becomes to build a world-class team.

Habit #8: Solution Orientation. Many people focus on the problem in front of them instead of the solution waiting to find them. (*Every* problem carries with it a solution, even if you can't see it right away.) This trait is due to the negativity bias of the human brain we explored earlier in our time together, a trait that served us well tens of thousands of years ago when each day provided deadly threats of starvation, or attack by animals or warring tribes. Money masters have patiently programmed themselves, through consistent daily practice, to constantly look for the opportunity within each difficulty and the solution inside every challenge. Do remember that a problem only becomes a problem when viewed as a problem.

Habit #9: Sustained Helpfulness. You now know well that money is the reward delivered for usefulness rendered. Barons pick businesses that raise the lives of billions of human beings. Which, in turn, makes them billions in income. It's very hard to have economic prosperity when you select an opportunity that offers little chance of impact.

Okay. Hope my sharing of these nine traits of top moguls is useful to your growth. I'll end this longer than usual chapter here as I promised my parents I'd call them. So I need to go call them. Let's talk later.

103

Develop The
Doubling Discipline

Another quality of the tycoons I advise is their near obsession with doubling their money as quickly as possible. When they consider a new opportunity, one of the first questions they ask is, "How great is the risk and how high is the upside, so I can, at the very least, double my capital?"

In financial circles, this kind of thinking is known as The Rule of 72, which says that at a return of 10 percent, it will take approximately seven years to double your money.

You see, the majority of people work for their money, trading their hours for income. But fortune-makers are very much about participating in projects that allow them to make money while they sleep. And compound massively over time. Definitely understand this as it's incredibly important—*they make their cash work for them.* (The habit is sometimes called The SWISS Method: Sales While I Sleep Soundly.)

Financially rich humans first learn the skill of making money and then the *separate* skill of multiplying that money by applying the Doubling Discipline. For example, under The Rule of 72, $100,000 turns into $200,000 in roughly seven years at a rate of 10 percent, $400,000 after fourteen years, $800,000 after twenty-one years, $1.6 million after twenty-eight years, $3.2 million after thirty-five years, $6.4 million after forty-two years, and so on, without any of your effort invested. You just sleep sweetly. And dream soundly.

Finally, money superstars exercise the third and completely different skill of *protecting* their financial wealth. It's one thing to make it and another thing to grow it and yet another thing to ensure you don't lose it. Without *each* of these three capabilities, they would never be where they are.

I'll leave you with these words of comedian Steve Martin:

> I love money. I love everything about it. I bought some pretty good stuff. Got a fur sink. An electric dog polisher. A gasoline powered turtleneck sweater. And, of course, I bought some dumb stuff too.

104

Translate Video-Watching into Fortune-Making

Here's a simple yet powerful idea to seriously raise the level of your prosperity in the fifth form of wealth: take most of the daily hours you spend watching online videos of little value and turn them into productivity that creates deep value for other human beings.

This could mean you use the time to read so you increase the knowledge and expertise you bring to your marketplace. Perhaps you'll apply this freed-up time to write more about your heroic ideals, most exciting goals and vividly imagined lifestyle in your journal. Or maybe you'll use the time you'd waste to turn up your fitness, pursue an extraordinary passion, or build better relationships.

You could deploy these extra hours to teach an online course on a subject you love (that just might end up helping hordes of people across the planet), make an app that disrupts an entire industry, launch a start-up that ignites a movement, or write a screenplay that delights humanity. Someone will do it, so why not you? And if not now, then when?

Even better, you could use the time you spent fooling around to go for a nature walk with your significant other, reach out to your parents, or have an interesting conversation with a lifetime friend.

Life passes in a blink. And the time we waste we never get back. Sure, playing with our digital devices can be fun now and then. Yet making your life gorgeous, prosperous, and honestly rich while you contribute to the welfare of the world is an even more joy-filled game.

105

Why Do It If It Doesn't Make You Happy?

Please don't send me a message that says, "Life is hard and it's easy for you and we have bills to pay and it's impossible to live life the way you suggest."

I get that life can be hard. I've suffered a lot more than you know.

And although it might surprise you, I too have bills to pay, a ton of obligations to fulfill, and more on my weary shoulders than you may imagine.

All I'm trying to say during this session is: Why do something if you don't love it?

I used to deliver speaking presentations for Fortune 500 clients across the globe that lasted an entire day. Toured the world, talking about leadership and mastering change and growing teams of top-performing Leaders Without Titles at every level of the organization, in big stadiums—for years.

Then I reached a place where those long hours on the platform stopped being fun. I actually started to dread having to present long into the afternoon, after a morning start.

One day over a long lunch in the sunshine of New York City, a friend said to me: "So why not build the rest of your speaking career around only doing the things you want to do?"

Game-changer. Life-shifting moment. Radical, simple, and very beautiful insight.

And so I did. (You have more power than you know and more choices than you think, even if you currently think you don't.)

I stopped accepting full-day invitations and returned to my true love: seventy-five-minute keynotes. The result? By declining 70 percent of incoming requests, I got my joy back. And guess what? Rather than losing invitations, far more requests came in.

I did the same thing in other areas of my business.

... I refused to work with people who drained my energy.

... I released suppliers who made excuses, brought me problems, and overpromised yet underdelivered.

... I avoided each and every pursuit that stained my happiness.

The fantastic and somewhat bizarre consequence of doing only that which fueled my joy (and that I was best at)?

Our enterprise grew. I attracted an even higher grade of client. New teammates who wanted to show up at mastery, operate with creativity, and join our mission to make our precious world a far more splendid place pounded on our doors.

My personal life dramatically increased in inspiration, enthusiasm, and freedom.

The valuable lesson for you? Create your career on *your* terms. Your days are too numbered to be unhappy.

105

Why Do It If It Doesn't Make You Happy?

Please don't send me a message that says, "Life is hard and it's easy for you and we have bills to pay and it's impossible to live life the way you suggest."

I get that life can be hard. I've suffered a lot more than you know.

And although it might surprise you, I too have bills to pay, a ton of obligations to fulfill, and more on my weary shoulders than you may imagine.

All I'm trying to say during this session is: Why do something if you don't love it?

I used to deliver speaking presentations for Fortune 500 clients across the globe that lasted an entire day. Toured the world, talking about leadership and mastering change and growing teams of top-performing Leaders Without Titles at every level of the organization, in big stadiums—for years.

Then I reached a place where those long hours on the platform stopped being fun. I actually started to dread having to present long into the afternoon, after a morning start.

One day over a long lunch in the sunshine of New York City, a friend said to me: "So why not build the rest of your speaking career around only doing the things you want to do?"

Game-changer. Life-shifting moment. Radical, simple, and very beautiful insight.

And so I did. (You have more power than you know and more choices than you think, even if you currently think you don't.)

I stopped accepting full-day invitations and returned to my true love: seventy-five-minute keynotes. The result? By declining 70 percent of incoming requests, I got my joy back. And guess what? Rather than losing invitations, far more requests came in.

I did the same thing in other areas of my business.

... I refused to work with people who drained my energy.

... I released suppliers who made excuses, brought me problems, and overpromised yet underdelivered.

... I avoided each and every pursuit that stained my happiness.

The fantastic and somewhat bizarre consequence of doing only that which fueled my joy (and that I was best at)?

Our enterprise grew. I attracted an even higher grade of client. New teammates who wanted to show up at mastery, operate with creativity, and join our mission to make our precious world a far more splendid place pounded on our doors.

My personal life dramatically increased in inspiration, enthusiasm, and freedom.

The valuable lesson for you? Create your career on *your* terms. Your days are too numbered to be unhappy.

106

Recruit a Dead Board of Directors

None of us can do it alone. Elite athletes all have coaches for a reason: to push them beyond their common limits so they achieve peak results. The first known use of the word "coach" as a guide can be found at Oxford University around 1830 and was slang for a tutor who carried a student (like in a horse-drawn coach) through a subject. And so, a coach is someone who transports an individual from a starting point in their learning to the place they wish to arrive.

A good one will encourage you to continue when you feel like stopping, save you time by showing you shortcuts to reach your goal, and hold you accountable so you don't come up with alibis for not doing the things you promised you'd do.

Of course, an excellent mentor comes with costs. And if you're in a situation where your budget doesn't allow for this monetary investment, I have a solution: instead of working with a life coach, seek a dead one. Yes, I'm serious.

I've had so many long-since-gone teachers who helped me profoundly that I can't remember them all. For years, I studied at the feet of Nelson Mandela for instruction on daily heroism, Roman emperor Marcus Aurelius for lifelong wisdom, Mother Teresa for guidance on servant leadership, William Shakespeare on craftsmanship, Benjamin Franklin on character building, Amelia Earhart on courage, the Spartan king Leonidas for turning trouble into triumph, Michelangelo for advice on artistry, Isaac Asimov for getting big things done (he wrote five hundred books in his lifetime, so I'm only an amateur), and Florence Scovel Shinn, Joseph Murphy, Maxwell Maltz, and Kahlil Gibran for their counsel on metaphysics and spirituality.

These individuals, and a vast array of other great human beings, have been for me a sort of Quiet Board of Advisors, through the insights offered in their memoirs or autobiographies, or in books inspired by their well-lived lives. May I gently suggest you find your Dead Board of Directors too.

107

Sit for Rich Ideas

In his valuable classic, *Think and Grow Rich*, author Napoleon Hill writes about an inventor who had an unusual practice that brought him a fortune.

The man had set up a room where he would go to "sit for ideas."

The room was sparse, containing only a table and a chair. The lights would be turned off and the inventor would enter the room, close his eyes and then wait for his creative intelligence to send him solutions to the biggest problems that he was trying to solve through his inventions.

In a time where so few of us are ever solitary (and even when we are, we are still with our phones), be one of those remarkable people who embrace the power of being alone and quiet.

Go to your place of peace. Shut the door. Turn off the lights. And sit for the ideas that will allow you to bring great solutions to people's pressing problems. Your creativity and ingenuity will be rewarded nicely.

Makes me think of what French mathematician Blaise Pascal once said: "All of humanity's problems stem from man's inability to sit quietly in a room alone." Good, right?

108

Bless Your Money Daily

I woke up later than usual this morning. None of that 5AM Club stuff! My recent workouts have been harder, so I needed more rest. And—of course—that's okay. Just don't fall into the trap of confusing laziness with recovery.

But allow me to get to the point. A few years back, in a dusty ancient bookshop in central London, I found a book called *Bring Out the Magic in Your Mind*. It was written many years ago by a man named Al Koran, who was then known as "the finest mental magician in the world." In a chapter called "The Secret of Wealth," he writes the following:

> When you send your money out, remember always to bless it. Ask it to bless everybody that it touches, and command it to go out and feed the hungry and clothe the naked and command it to come back to you one million-fold. Don't pass over this lightly.

Over the next few days, why not apply this author's strange yet fascinating advice? And see what happens.

When you pay for your groceries, silently bless all those who have helped bring this food to you: the farmers who have grown it, the laborers who have picked it, the truckers who have transported it, and the cashiers who have sold it.

If you're writing a check for car repairs, why not give silent appreciation to all the factory workers who made the part, the delivery people who carried it, and the mechanics who got your car working again?

When you buy a book from a bookstore, bless the bookseller, and when you enjoy a cup of coffee, glorify the barista. You get my drift. Just become an unlimited, highly enthusiastic gratefulness spreader. To uplift lives. And to increase your wealth.

As the timeless truth teaches us, the hand that gives, gathers.

109

Being Good
Is Good Business

Yesterday I delivered a keynote for an enthusiastic group of eleven thousand top leaders in São Paulo. I spoke about the importance of leveraging high-velocity change for exponential success. I shared that the bigger the dream, the more essential the team. I noted that the best leaders grow more leaders and are servant heroes, putting the growth and welfare of their people above the needs of their egos. And I offered the idea that the wiser, braver, healthier, and more decent we make ourselves as people, the more superb will be our results in business. Because what happens within determines what unfolds without. And to change the world we must start by improving ourselves.

A very polite and well-dressed man in a crisp gray suit with black shoes that shone like a perfect summer day came up to me after the presentation and asked if I had a few minutes to answer a question.

"Sure, how can I help?" I replied.

"Private equity has invested in my company. I need to grow profits quickly to keep them happy. I like your idea of acting in a way that's good for society as well as good for our firm, what you said about 'linking paycheck to purpose' and how world-class leaders 'find a cause that's larger than themselves.' Yet it's not really practical. I'm sorry to say this to you, Robin."

Hmmm. Being a person of vast integrity, impeccable honesty, strong character virtues, and a noble heart isn't just good for your soul. It's absolutely fantastic for the economic engine of your business. Actually, I can't think of a better competitive advantage than being someone whom people deeply respect and totally trust.

Being good is good business. And excellent things happen to leaders who do excellent things.

Being the kind of person who viscerally believes in your crusade and will do whatever it takes to take wonderful care of the people around you—while helping the dreams of your customers come true—will pretty much guarantee that your reputation will rise, your team will remain loyal, and your customers will shift from regular clients to *fanatical followers*. Who are so inspired and delighted by you and your team they tell everyone they know about what you do.

Of course, this will increase the bottom line. *Dramatically*.

The gentleman's comment contained an assumption: that working with less ego, more honor, and greater devotion to benefiting others would decrease the money he'd make. Wrong.

Just the opposite is the truth. Serving with magnificence, grace, mastery, and dignity will make him rich, financially as well as spiritually.

Leading with caring, authenticity, decency, and love (there, I said it!) causes your team, customers, suppliers and investors to fall in love with you. And to do whatever they can to protect you.

People do business with people they like. Humans give business to people they trust. And all of us want to offer our loyalty to individuals who make us feel special.

I mentioned much of this to the man at my leadership presentation. He nodded sincerely. I'm not sure he totally agreed with me. Then he shook my hand and walked off into the dense crowd.

110

Be a Highly Humble Leader

The thing about a master is they always think they are an apprentice. And the thing about a professional is they keep the mindset of an amateur, always hungry to learn, improve, and evolve. We visited this concept before. Yet it's essential that I reinforce it for you. So that you remember it, after our time together is over.

Becoming an expert in your field is dangerous. Why? For the reason that experts fall into the trap of believing they know everything. They develop a huge sense of pride in all they know. So they stop being willing to change their minds. So they stop studying, preparing, working, innovating, and optimizing. So they rest on their laurels and think that because they're at the top they'll automatically remain at the top. This arrogance is the beginning of their end.

I encourage you to do whatever it takes to insulate your humbleness as you rise in the success that will attract more money to you. *Humility is necessary for enduring mastery.* And the greatest leaders don't think too much of themselves. I'm not at all saying not to have high self-worth. I'm just saying—in this culture of too many people tooting their own horns and trumpeting their own genius—be quiet. And stay open.

Now, you might not think you're a leader, but in fact you very much are. Years ago, I wrote a book called *The Leader Who Had No Title*. Really, you can lead without a position, influence without an office, and impact without formal authority.

When one of my kids was little, I asked them what it meant to be a leader. The reply was unforgettable: "Dad, at school, when we all have to walk to the playground, the person at the front of the line is the leader. But the cool thing is that every day, someone new gets to stand at the front of the line. So everyone in the class gets their turn to be a leader."

But leading without a title isn't the main point of this mentoring message. My key here is to gently remind you to be humble in the skills you pursue, work you do and life you make. *Because the humblest is the greatest.*

Which brings me to a story I've never forgotten about Konosuke Matsushita, the founder of Panasonic, the global electronics company.

One day, he was set to have a meal at a steak restaurant in the heart of Tokyo. The staff at the restaurant were on high alert and their best behavior, knowing that one of the icons of Japanese business would be visiting their place.

With the eyes of everyone in the room on him, the luminary of industry was carefully served a perfect steak, painstakingly prepared by the eminent chef. Matsushita ate part of the steak that had been made for him. But then left most of it.

Those who watched from the kitchen appeared distressed and slightly heartbroken. They felt they had failed to impress their revered guest. And took it as a personal defeat that they had failed to deliver.

The grandmaster of commerce asked to speak to the chef, which made the team even more nervous. All thought jobs would be lost and reputations ruined.

Yet something completely different happened.

After the chef came out of the kitchen, Matsushita said, with his head held low, in an aged and whispery voice, "Please forgive me. Your food was superb. I'm an old man so I don't eat that much anymore. I just wanted to let you know this so you don't think that I didn't enjoy your exquisite food. I thank you. And I thank your fine team for your generous hospitality."

As you lead without a title and create the financial fortune that feels truest and most honest to you, I champion you to keep your feet on the ground. As you rise, grow even more modest. Even more willing to learn. Listen. Invent. Optimize. Serve. And never, ever show off. It's bad manners. And degrading to your greatness.

Do all that I'm suggesting and you'll be assured of being at the top for a long time. And one of the primary goals when it comes to success isn't just to reach it. It's to sustain it. Ordinary producers aspire to reach the peak. Legends are dedicated to remaining there for an entire career. So the generations who follow them know that they were there.

My beloved father used to say this: "Robin, the tree that bears the most fruit bows overs the most." Please think about that over the hours ahead. Even in a society with people going out of their way to show you how smart, strong and rich they are, be a humble leader. And a grounded human being.

111

The Investment with The Highest Return

Equities, precious metals, treasury bills, and real estate. These are where those who invest their money commonly land.

Fine. Yet if you are serious about a major return on your investment, then I recommend that you invest far more in yourself. Building your best you is your best investment, by a huge factor.

It's now popular to call it "self-care." Or classify it as "personal development." Or categorize it as "human optimization." No matter how you label it, investing your focus, energy, knowledge, and time into elevating your Mindset (your psychology), purifying your Heartset (your emotionality), calibrating your Healthset (your physicality), and upgrading your Soulset (your spirituality)—what you now know as The 4 Interior Empires from my methodology—is absolutely, unquestionably, and indisputably the *finest* investment you can make. The one that yields the highest returns.

Improving your Mindset via reading, affirming, planning, and

MVP (Meditation, Visualization, and Prayer) each morning will dramatically raise your mental concentration, your creativity, your positivity, your resilience, and your productivity, as well as your overall sense of peacefulness (and nothing will cost you more than losing your peace of mind).

Increasing the wellness of your Heartset through gratitude, periods of silence, journaling, working with a therapist, receiving regular bodywork, walking in nature, and hypnosis (as some examples) will significantly enrich your personal and professional relationships (because your emotional intelligence soars and your empathy for others shines), cause you to be far less reactive in stressful times, turn pain into power and transmute fear into multiple forms of fortune.

Raising the fitness of your Healthset through a daily, sweaty, early morning workout, eating cleanly, supplementing correctly, carefully exploring fasting, sunbathing (in moderation), getting fresh air, napping, and sleeping richly will cause explosive gains in your energy, stamina, happiness, and performance, as well as noticeably extend your lifespan.

And intensifying the intimacy with your Soulset through the work of worship, spending time in careful contemplation, studying inspiring books, writing about who you wish to become, and being useful to others grows your personal heroism and expands your wisdom wonderfully.

So I need to repeat it to reinforce it: Your life always reflects *you*. As you rise, your outer conditions increase to match your new level of human greatness. I know this might sound esoteric and not practical. But it's oh-so-practical. Make *you* better and your income, influence and impact get (a whole lot) better.

Our culture teaches us the opposite. We are schooled into believing that when we get the worldly victories, we'll somehow wake up feeling victorious as people. Not true.

The doorway to success swings inward, not outward. When you make the investment to create a majestic inner life by tending to The 4 Interior Empires daily, your exterior results will offer you an exquisite return.

112

Ask The Billion-Dollar Business Question

There's a question I've recommended that my clients ask their customers often. It's a simple one. One that has made them, collectively, billions of dollars. I'll share it with you, in the spirit of helpfulness. It goes like this:

"Thank you for telling me what you liked about your experience with us. Now, please tell me what you *didn't like* and, if you were in my shoes, how would you go about making things great?"

Really so simple. Yet honestly so extremely valuable. Trust me on this.

It's very rare for a businessperson to have the guts to ask for feedback and constructive input from the very individuals consuming their products and services, even though this information is the pure gold that will make them and their shop better, more successful, and more enduring.

Oh, and after you've asked the question, *listen*. I watch many people rush to rationalize why there were problems and make excuses as soon as the customer starts giving the feedback asked for. Don't do that. Just ask the question and go completely quiet so your buyer can share all the insights that will—once acted on—take your business to a completely new level of success. And after you fully hear their first answer, then say "And what else?" so your customer shares more and more of the extremely precious information.

The Billion-Dollar Business Question borders on magic. Why? Because most of us suffer from a dreaded affliction called fear of rejection. We only want to hear the positive. A consumer may share what they liked about doing business with you (because most human beings hate conflict, they'll tell you about the good things that you want to hear) and then leave, never to return (if there were bad parts of their customer experience). Then they will go tell all their neighbors and thousands of virtual friends what they didn't like—destroying your reputation and brand in the process. If you go no deeper than listening for the positive, you'll miss all the treasure.

113

Silently Adore Your Haters

Yes. I'm strange. I've not only encouraged you to bless your money, I'm now going to push you to adore your haters.

I cherish my competitors and I appreciate my hurters and I salute my criticizers (not that I have many of them, thankfully).

I really do love the concept of *namaste* that is so traditional in India, on meeting another person. The hands clasped together is a gesture that means "I bow to the divine within you." Imagine bowing to the divine (and the gifts and goodness) that exists in *everyone*? (Although I agree that they seem locked away in some.)

I often wake up with a quick prayer for the health and happiness of my family, friends, team, and beloved readers.

And then I move on to blessing those who were there for me when I was down. Those who helped me when I was hurt. Those who stood by me in the storms and fires.

I continue the routine by blessing my clients, my neighbors and my fellow citizens. I'll even bless a room before I go into it and an audience before I take the stage. So everyone I encounter feels my positive vibes and encouraging energy.

Here's the thing, though: I also send my finest wishes to the not-so-worthy ones. The naysayers, the trolls, the takers, and the ones who do not wish me well.

I silently send light, love, and a sincere prayer of good wishes to those who have caused me grief, those who did me wrong, and those who have tried their best to make my life miserable.

This blessing makes me stronger. It helps them grow wiser. And I do believe that if we all did this every morning our planet would be a brighter place.

114

Greedy Is Not Happy

The man on the private jet who can't sleep until he has three more. The woman who owns an entire island yet won't feel fulfilled until she acquires all the surrounding ones. The business sovereign who has a billion yet needs ten. You know what I call them? Addicts.

And you know what someone who has so much yet sees it as not a lot is called? Greedy, greedy, greedy.

It's so very easy to think that these people who have plenty materially are happy, happy, happy.

Greedy people are never happy, no matter what their outward-facing lives look like. It may seem to the onlooker that they have it all and live in an enchanted way.

Most are miserable, actually. Why, you ask? Because nothing is ever enough for them. And as soon as they reach one summit, they anxiously start climbing the next one. They never enjoy and savor the fruits of their labor. Everything's a race. It's all a competition to be better than another. One long contest in striving and out-winning everyone else.

This is not a wise or successful or peaceful way to live. Avoid it at all costs. Please.

115

Go Relational, Not Transactional

"Take care of the relationship and the money will take care of itself" is a mantra worth reciting (and then underlining).

Too many businesses are about the cash grab instead of the long term.

A start-up tycoon that I mentor (he became an UHNWI—an ultra-high-net-worth individual—in under twelve months) shared that he recently went into a well-known restaurant in a city loved by tourists. Within five minutes of entering, he was pestered for his order. And within ten minutes, food was in front of him so they could soon turn the table for another customer.

Of course, he'll never return. Ever. Just think about the income the restaurant would have made having my client, his family, and his friends in there consistently. Over months, years, and decades, it would add up to many tens of thousands. If not more (he loves expensive red wine).

He just moved to that city, and told me that if they had treated him well, he would have eaten there a few times a week. And tipped like a king.

All lost! Because the owner was more focused on making transactions than on forging good relationships with the human beings who made the choice to show up at his restaurant. He treated people as a commodity rather than seeing growing personal connections as an opportunity (that would bring happiness to himself and others—along with raising his sales).

Every single person alive today is wearing an invisible badge that screams "make me feel important." In this age of machines, we all long for rich human contact, a place where we have a sense of belonging and simple kindness. Operating like this is good for your income. And wonderful for your well-being.

116

My Top 10 Books for Prosperity

When a billionaire-level client shows me their library (after a dinner together, they often invite me to continue the conversation in this room of their home), the top ten books I most often see (or that they tell me helped them most in the building of their economic empire) are the following:

As You Think by James Allen
Think and Grow Rich by Napoleon Hill
How to Win Friends and Influence People by Dale Carnegie
The Richest Man in Town by Randall Jones
The Millionaire Fastlane by MJ DeMarco
How to Attract Money by Joseph Murphy
The Ten Roads to Riches by Ken Fisher
The Magic of Thinking Big by David Schwartz
How to Get Rich by Felix Dennis
The Seven Spiritual Laws of Success by Deepak Chopra

Definitely read each one of them. And remember that the leader who learns the most, wins.

117

To Make a Million, Help a Million

A number of shifts will significantly increase the money flow in your life . . .

. . . to release your history and thereby rewrite your destiny.

. . . to leap from constant entertainment to consistent education.

. . . to rise from endless busyness to slow, focused, and rich productivity.

. . . from competing with others to running the race against your former self.

Yet when it comes to building financial wealth, few shifts are as potent as being less of a consumer and more of a creator. Bernard Arnault, one of the planet's most economically rich people, said: "Money is just a consequence. Don't worry about profitability. Do your job well. Make the lives of others better. Profitability will come."

To put it even more clearly for you: every empire-maker makes the things the majority consumes. (Read that one twice, I do suggest.)

You see, the bigger the problem you solve, the more people you'll help. And as you know so well: the money is the reward for value delivered—and magic rendered to the marketplace. To make a million, serve a million. To become a billionaire, help one billion people.

And that requires you to neglect your social media feed, stop watching low-value videos, and make something that matters.

Less consumption. Less buying every attractive object. Less filling our homes and storage lockers with things we really don't need and never truly liked. And, instead, positively creating, building, and generating something from your brave idea, native talent, and awesome sweat equity.

This is why you can actually choose to see increasing your financial wealth as a spiritual pursuit. Sincerely serving other human beings with mastery, ingenuity, and excellence enriches their lives, introduces you to your hidden talents and gifts, lowers the problems of the world (via innovation), gives you a deep sense of meaning, and raises your financial freedom in the process. How perfect!

Perhaps these words of Steve Jobs are a good way for us to close out this section on the fifth form of wealth. He said, "Being the richest person in the cemetery doesn't matter to me. Going to bed at night saying we've done something wonderful, that's what matters to me."

THE 6TH FORM OF WEALTH

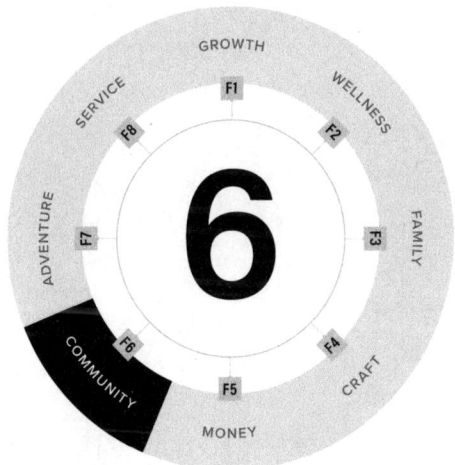

Community

The You Become Your Social Network Habit

Intelligent people tend to have less friends than the average person. The smarter you are, the more selective you become.
—Nikola Tesla

The 6th Form of Wealth
Community | Quick Overview

Community, to me, isn't simply about your neighborhood and the area where you live, shop, dine and walk. I use the term, in the section we're about to explore together, to describe your wider social clan and the human tribe that are essential to the making of a meaningful, cheerful, and rich existence.

The common proverb "your network determines your net worth" needs to be adjusted to add that your community and associations also increase your *self-worth*. The more good and amazing people you have in your personal circle, the better you'll feel about yourself—and all you can do, have and become in your lifetime.

Multiple rewards flow to you when you invest in the currency of an exceptionally good social orbit. You'll be elevated by the superb examples set by others. You'll always have a great group of human beings to support, encourage, and champion you. You'll have constant help when you need it and a group of individuals who you can count on when you least expect it. Doors that were previously closed will be opened for you (because your friends and alliances all have their friends and alliances) and opportunities for greater success start appearing, as others begin to introduce you to their web of trusted people. As well, just being emotionally connected with splendid souls will make your days far happier, healthier, more satisfying—and more colorful.

It really does take just a single conversation with an inspiring or wise or deeply compassionate individual to change the way you see the world and reorder how you show up in it. So select the people who populate your social network well. It's an essential form of wealth. And your richest life depends on this.

118

Choose a Brighter Neighborhood

If you're the most curious, enthusiastic, and happy person on your street, maybe it's time to move to a new street. If you're the smartest person you know, maybe—just maybe—it's time to know new people. If you're the most visionary and creative person in your social circle, perhaps it's time to reconstruct your circle. And if you're the wisest, bravest, and most kind person in your whole neighborhood, then I really do think it's time for you to move. To an entirely new neighborhood.

Just saying. You'll always play better when you play with better players, right?

One of my favorite films is *Burnt*. It's about a bad boy Michelin two-star chef with personal demons, a man who was once the darling of the Paris restaurant landscape but whose drug habit forced him to depart for the wilderness of a less sensational place, where he shucked one million oysters as his chosen form of penance.

In one scene, the culinary superstar is in the kitchen of his archrival who—in a rare moment of vulnerability—admits: "You're better than me. Which makes you the best. The rest of us need you to lead us to places we wouldn't otherwise go."

To know *real* fortune, you really must surround yourself with *great* people. Befriend people who think, produce, live, and love better than you. People who will lead you to places you would not visit. And lift you to levels you wouldn't otherwise reach.

119

Live Your Hero's Life

I like to ask the leaders I work with this question to upgrade and refine the universe of their relationships: "If anything was possible, whose life would you love to be living?"

The answer always brings their ideal social network—and personal lifestyle—into sharper focus, since the people around us are superb examples of the results that are available to us.

Please pause for a moment and answer the question yourself. Would you like to be Rosa Parks for a day or Rembrandt for a week? How about Alexander the Great for a month or Joan of Arc for a year?

Maybe you'd like to test out the life of Martin Luther King Jr. or JFK or Mr. Mandela or Mahatma Gandhi? Perhaps you'll get all fired up thinking about spending the rest of your days like Rockefeller or Sam Walton, Michelangelo or Harper Lee, the pop star named Prince or the musical artist named Gaga.

I'm not sure who you'd dream of becoming, if you and I were sitting together on the terrace of my farmhouse in the Tuscan sunshine talking about your future. What I do know is this: Your thinking really is a self-fulfilling prophecy. And you'll never reach a result that you haven't even considered.

120

Do What You Say You'll Do

Fairly quick message for you: when you tell someone—anyone—in your community that you'll do something, do it! So simple. So rare. You'll become dependable, credible and unbelievably unforgettable to everyone you interact with. You'll stand out rather than fitting in, like a cog in the machine or a follower of the herd.

. . . Say you'll follow up with a work prospect, then contact them at the exact moment you promised you would.

. . . Tell a friend you'll take them to dinner for their birthday, then book the restaurant and actually take them out for their treat.

. . . Mention to your mate or child that you'll do something special with them one evening, then plan the outing with great care, schedule the event (because the things that get scheduled are the things that get done) and then follow through by bringing them there.

Yes! Become a Grandmaster of Following Through and a Wizard of Keeping Your Word.

It's just too common to see people breaking their promises. It's easy to have such a full plate of commitments that you fall into overwhelm and you just can't honor your pledge. May I humbly suggest that you make it a daily practice not to overpromise. Instead, underpromise. And then overdeliver. With each person you are blessed to have in your circle.

121

Start a Mastermind Alliance

One of the methods that has served me amazingly well is having a mastermind alliance. This is a group of two or more people who meet regularly to share their progress on key projects, encourage, each other to go farther, offer solutions to challenging problems and engage in the interesting conversations that push the growth that makes your days greater.

For years, every Friday at 6 AM I'd meet my mastermind partner at a coffee shop where we'd chat for about two hours. Sometimes we'd bring books we loved—to give to each other—or share written plans with our goals for learning new things, becoming physically fitter, launching new creative projects, or starting new spiritual pursuits.

Our sessions had laughter, storytelling, and—when we were passing through a hard season of life—even tears. I came to treasure these Friday morning meetings with my mastermind partner (we later switched from the coffee shop to a forest where we would walk the trails while talking). I loved what I learned, am grateful for the encouragement I received, and still remember how good these times made me feel, talking with a kindred spirit who just happened to see the world as I did.

Definitely start your mastermind alliance. In a year you will have wished you began it today. So why not begin it today?

122

The Stephen King Lost Letters Rule

Thank you notes, written with sincerity and appreciation, just might have the potential to change the world. I'm serious.

I send thank you notes all the time. On good stationery. Written in ink. Some take me half an hour to write because I think them through so much. I remember a CEO who made it a habit to send out five thousand Christmas cards every December. He'd start the process in June. People could sense how beautifully he valued them. The titan is one of the wealthiest people I know, financially, socially, internally, and spiritually.

I bought a treadmill to run on at home. It works unbelievably well. So I wrote a note to the head of the company that made it. To thank him for helping me stay fit and run strong. And putting such a glorious product out into the universe.

I ate at a special restaurant a few weeks ago. It was a simple place that offered local ingredients cooked over a fire. Magic! I was so impressed that I sent the chef a thank you note. Appreciating him for making my life a little better, by making mesmerizing food.

I'm reading *The Stories of My Life*, a memoir by the bestselling novelist James Patterson. In a chapter called "The Murder of Stephen King," Patterson explains how he wrote a short story with that title. King's people said, "Don't publish it." They felt it would jeopardize King's safety. (King's wife, Tabitha, had once faced an intruder who broke into their home.)

Patterson complied. His publisher, Little, Brown and Company, pulled *the entire print run*. The author then added, "And nobody ever sent a note of thanks. I guess he has trouble with thank you notes."

Send thank you notes to people who do good things. To show your gratefulness. To make their lives nicer. And to make yours much richer.

123

Karma Is Not Mystical, It's Practical

The adage "Let karma do your dirty work and let success be your revenge" is a powerful and practical one. (Not that I'm the slightest bit interested in revenge; what a complete waste of attention, energy and time.)

I've been on the planet long enough to know that good things happen to people who do good things. And not-so-great circumstances eventually show up for those who mistreat others. (By the way, every individual who has caused you pain will—sooner or later—feel embarrassed, ashamed, or sad about what they did to you; trust me on this.)

Anyway, the universe has a well-ordered accounting system, so always play fair, be honest, and treat each and every human being in your social sphere with the respect they deserve. Put out decency and generosity, and that's what will show up for you in return. To get respect you need to give it, right?

Practical (and easy) ways to get the wonders of karma working in your favor to build the wealth of community into your days include:

... Leave great tips for room cleaners at hotels. This is someone's father or mother, and their work is not easy.

... Leave your tray at the food court in your local mall at the place where you're supposed to, and keep it neat.

... If you're out on a nature walk and you see some trash, pick it up. Never, ever miss an opportunity to show some personal leadership and an unusual amount of integrity.

... Return anything you borrow (whether a book, a sweater, some cash or a favor). You cannot put a price tag on the value of your good name.

... When you park in a public parking spot (if you drive), position your car in such a way as to let others park next to you (I see many motorists taking up two or three spaces nowadays).

... Be the first to say sorry if you've made a mistake because it's better to be happy in all your relationships than constantly right.

Yes, treat people the way you wish people would treat you. "We have committed the Golden Rule to memory; let us now commit it to life," noted American poet Edwin Markham. Once you do—with the consistency that is the mother of mastery—the gold that is a deep, wide, and wonderful relationship network will shimmer like a shooting star, on the clearest summer night.

124

Remember The Vanishing Loved Ones Law

Confession: I not only love my family members, I also love my close friends, the amazing people I'm delighted to work with on my team, the clients who engage me for coaching, the companies that book me for keynote presentations and the readers who have allowed me the honor of writing books for over a quarter of a century.

I operate under a rule that has served me so well that I invite you to embrace it: *Treat everyone you meet like you might never see them again.* Because accidents happen, loss occurs, and emergencies are a part of life.

When you're with those you love (or like), be present and be real and be totally alive—instead of on your phone. (Never check your digital devices when you have a human being in front of you. It's not cool; it's rude.) Because people die when you least expect it. Or, less dramatically, coworkers move on, life partners get old, and children grow up. Most of us take the people closest to us for granted until we lose them.

A story. There was a very special man with a fascinating mind, strong character, and large heart who would transport me to a cottage that I'd go to write at, in a country that I found profoundly inspiring. On a recent visit, a new face was there to greet me.

I asked where my friend was. "He couldn't be here," was the reply. Then the new person took a long pause and said: "He passed away a few months ago. He was fishing one day and suddenly fell to the ground. Never woke up. We're all still in shock. He was only thirty-seven."

So remember that life can have its changes and that people can suddenly vanish. To enrich your community and add true wealth to your hours, treat everyone in it amazingly well. A time will come in the future where you'll be ever so glad that you did.

125

Why Have an Enemy When You Can Make a Friend?

I couldn't sleep the other night after a flight to Delhi, so I watched the film *King Arthur*. I learned a big lesson that I'd like to share with you today.

Essentially, it's this: *Why have an enemy when you can make a friend?*

I'm now in London as I write you this mentoring note. In a light-filled and quirkily designed hotel room with Pavarotti playing. I visited the Tate Modern yesterday (one of my all-time favorite art galleries), walked for hours along the River Thames, then had a good meal with an old friend (actually, he's not that old).

In life and at work, things happen, don't they? Conflict occurs. People do bad things. Things that end up causing you pain. And grief.

My recommendation to you is, first, forgive them. Their behavior made sense to them in that moment. If they had higher consciousness they would have acted better. So, yes, forgive them. And know that forgiving someone's bad behavior doesn't mean you forget it. Forgiving conduct has nothing to do with condoning conduct. It just means you understand that they did the best they could, with what they knew. And you are, therefore, able to let it go. And move on with your precious life. Because life is for the living.

My second suggestion is to forgive *yourself*. You're human and if ruminating over what they did frustrates, saddens, disappoints, or angers you, this is absolutely okay. And normal. The key is to feel those feelings so you can then be in a position to release those feelings, so you don't become an injustice collector, carrying years of irritations that block your energy, creativity, productivity, and happiness.

The real lesson here? Don't be in the habit of making enemies. And definitely don't be in the business of burning bridges.

It always surprises me how many people—when something doesn't go their way—act unwisely, emotionally and reactively, burning a bridge instead of building a gateway. Instead, when someone has disappointed you, use every opportunity (or at least most of them) to create a friend. Fascinating way to make your life better, right?

Yes, even one enemy is one too many. In all these years of my Earthwalk, I must tell you that I've only met about three truly nasty people (people I would never, ever allow into my life again). Really. Only about three.

Most people are just trying to get through their day. Hurt people hurt people. People in pain do painful things. Be the bigger person. Give them a second chance and see what they do. Generally, they will surprise you. And if they don't, you can still be their friend, from afar.

126

Be a Major Gift Giver

I need to tell you a secret: one of my favorite things to do is to give people gifts. I just love it! To be generous and caring and to put smiles on people's faces is one of the highest joys of my life. And I've realized that although my presents are not given with the hope of receiving a gift in return, generosity is a form of seed-planting. The most surprising rewards will come your way when you commit to being a regular giver.

When I was about six or seven years old, I adored a TV show called *Mr. Dressup*. The program ran for almost thirty years and was inspired by the renowned children's series *Mister Rogers' Neighborhood*.

Mr. Dressup (played by actor Ernie Coombs) had two best friends: a puppet child named Casey and a puppet dog named Finnegan—who, now that I think about it, looks a little like my dog SuperChum.

When the puppeteer who controlled Casey and Finnegan decided to leave due to her concerns that children's television was becoming too commercial, Mr. Dressup told his audience that his two buddies were no longer on the show because they went off to kindergarten.

And when it came time for his final show, he didn't tell all the kids who revered the series it was the last episode. Instead, he adjusted his usual sign-off with, "We end each show by saying, 'We have to go now. We'll see you again soon!' This last time that will be a lie."

One day when I was a boy, I scribbled a heartfelt and long letter to Mr. Dressup, letting him know how much he, Casey, and Finnegan meant to me. Guess what? A week later, a postcard with a picture of the three of them showed up in my mailbox. On the other side was a warm note from the mentor who had taught me so much about life. As a little kid.

Over fifty years after receiving that gift—from a person who took the time to send a kind note to a little kid—I still remember the postcard. And the gesture from Mr. Coombs.

... If I have an interesting conversation with a taxi driver, I'll ask him to write his name and address on a piece of paper. And then, *instantly* (so I don't postpone and possibly forget), I shoot a photo of the details using my phone camera and send them to my trusted executive assistant, Angela, with a request to mail the driver one of my books.

... If I have a neat chat with the barista in a coffee shop, I'll often walk to a nearby bookshop, buy one of my favorite books, such as *Meditations* by the Roman emperor Marcus Aurelius, *The Giving Tree* by Shel Silverstein, or *The Catcher in the Rye* by J. D. Salinger, and walk back to present it to them (with a nice inscription inside).

... If I connect with the doorman of a hotel I'm staying at (which I often do), I'll find a good wine shop and bring them back a lovely bottle of wine. To enjoy with their family.

... If a sales clerk at a shop is great at what they do, full of positivity and overflowing with caring, I'll go buy a bag of treats and return to offer it to them. (I'll keep a little for myself.)

As the French Quaker and missionary Étienne de Grellet observed, "I shall pass through this world but once; any good thing therefore that I can do, or any kindness that I can show to any fellow-creature, let me do it now. Let me not defer or neglect it, for I shall not pass this way again." Lovely.

127

Increase Your Charisma

I just read about bank collapses, more protests out on the streets and an earthquake that cost many beautiful human lives. All the volatility in our world worries me. Yet I also know it's in the most difficult times that true heroes emerge (so be one). As the writer Christopher Morley said, "You can curse the darkness or light a candle."

Your passion is contagious and your personal energy can be magnetic if you do the right things. Please remember that you have more magic within you than you are currently experiencing. Here are seven ways to raise your charisma factor so you bring more inspiration to the world (and develop an even better social network):

Use people's names. This is an utterly underrated way to genuinely build rapport with someone you seek to connect with. The psychological reality is that people feel happy at the sound of their names. It makes them feel seen, valued, and special.

Be on time. It's better to be an hour early than a minute late. The ritual of punctuality sends a strong signal to the other person that they are respected. When you are on time, you show that you value the time of the person that you're meeting. And demonstrate that you're not a flake.

Have beautiful manners. Oh, how inspirational it is to watch one of those rare-air leaders who display perfect manners. It makes them stand out, exude grace, and rise above the pack, where a lack of civility is as common as the air we breathe.

Smile sincerely. A human smile is a supreme connection accelerator. And a trust activator. No matter where you go in the world, even if you don't speak the language, you can make friends and influence people sincerely and with integrity by giving them an honest grin. So do it more often. With practice, you'll become your local smile master.

Be more interested than interesting. I'll repeat this to reinforce it: You'll never express the fullness of your natural charisma and leave people better than you found them if you're so insecure that your main aim is to hog the spotlight. In a world of loud talkers, be a quiet leader. In an age of glitzy influencers, become the most generous person you know. I know it's counterintuitive, but the more you shine a light on others, the more the light will shine all over you.

Be vulnerable. The philosopher Marshall McLuhan observed, "That which is most personal is most universal." When you expose your scars and share your struggles, people begin to believe in you. They relate to you. You give them permission to be real. And deep bonds are developed.

Be an original. Steve Jobs' turtlenecks. Anna Wintour's large sunglasses. Niki Lauda's red baseball cap. Warren Buffett's hamburgers. Mahatma Gandhi's loincloth. These are all examples of accessories used by standouts to, well, stand out. When done with authenticity and honesty, dressing or behaving in a way that is different from the majority, yet most true to you, significantly elevates your charisma. And makes you unforgettable in your field.

By the way, this talk of originality makes me think of a story of something that happened at a tea party in honor of King George V at Buckingham Palace. A reporter—looking at Mahatma Gandhi in his loincloth and sandals—asked, "Mr. Gandhi, do you think you are properly dressed to meet the king?"

The great hero's reply was spectacular: "Do not worry about my clothes. The king has enough on for both of us."

Elle and I are going into the local village for a nice long lunch of burrata and pasta. So I should end this message right here. Thanks for being so open to all I'm offering. I really do think you're something special. Ciao.

128

Go See People in Person

At a time of nonstop online interactions, I strongly recommend that you maximize all opportunity for human connection, in person.

I find it fascinating that we've never been so able to be united virtually, yet so many good souls among us have never been so lonely. It's common to have a few hundred cyberfriends, yet much less common to have three friends you meet regularly for coffee or tea.

Once I read of a woman who would regularly fly ten tours for a sixty-minute meeting. "Relationships are built by breaking bread together and connecting face to face," she noted.

In Italy they say, "We are not friends until we've eaten together." Wisdom, yes?

Magic often happens when we gather, shake hands, look into eyes, feel the energy, sense the chemistry, and build the unity that creates special results.

Given this, put down your phone, go offline, put on your coat, go for a walk. And interact with someone—in person.

129

You Never Know Who Someone Will Become

I'm in Baku, Azerbaijan, today, working on this section of the book. Writing in my hotel room. The general manager left me a note for my arrival, next to a bowl of fruit.

The message was cryptic. It said, "We met twenty years ago. I'll tell you about it when we meet. Your fan, Bob."

I called him nearly instantly. Curious to know what he was referring to. He was super warm on the phone. Very polite. Invited me for tea.

As we spoke in the elegant breakfast restaurant of the property, he told me that his first job was in banquet services at a small hotel in a tiny city. When I first started out as a speaker, I'd run my workshops there (twenty-three people showed up to my first one; twenty-one of them were family members). Staff would wheel out a television to show my slides (yes, a television!). It was amateurish. Beginner level. But it was my start, so I must celebrate it.

Bob worked hard, did his work extremely well, and rose to become the banquet manager. When we met for tea, he explained that even though he was in management, he cared so much about how my workshops went that it was he who would bring in the television we'd use. Twenty years ago, wheeling out the TV.

And now here he was. The GM of the super-stylish and absolutely marvelous Four Seasons Hotel in Baku. Dressed impeccably and a pillar of the community.

I kept his generous note. Slipped it into my journal, actually. To remind me of the power of human connections in a world gone too digital. I'd been fortunate to meet a person who remembered the importance of small acts of bonding and simple feats of caring. Thank you, dear Bob. I will always wish you well.

His gesture inspired me to write four letters on the stationery that good hotels such as his still provide. One to my parents, thanking them for their influence and all the amazing things they've done for me over my lifetime (thanks for having me, Mom and Dad!). One to Elle, appreciating her limitless love and endless encouragement through thick and thin. And two to my beloved children who bring me such joy.

Maybe even more essentially, his note reminded me to treat every single person you meet with the utmost of respect, politeness, and kindness. Not only is this way of rolling through the rest of your life good for your conscience and great for your happiness, it's fantastic for the building of your social circle. Because you never know who someone will become.

130

Wish People a Great Day

I agree the title of this chapter reflects a basic idea, yet you don't see it in real life all that often: wish people a great day.

This morning, after a visit to the gym, I stopped at a shop and picked up a bottle of water and a berry and hibiscus kombucha.

I complimented the young woman behind the counter on the range of goods, which spanned from unusual protein bars to one of the most amazing croissants I'd ever seen (I passed on buying one, yet I still wake up at night in a hot sweat after dreaming about the darn thing).

She thanked me for the appreciation in a very wonderful way. And then I paid for my drinks.

Before I left, I said, "Have a great day." It made her smile. She paused—looking at me intently. Then she replied, "You have a good day too."

It takes so little to lift someone's mood. To show them some goodness. And to help a person remember that they matter. "Be kind, for everyone you meet is fighting a hard battle," wrote the Scottish author Ian Maclaren.

I honestly believe that giving someone a lively and fully present greeting on meeting them—and wishing them a brilliant rest of their day on leaving them—will make our world easier for all. Definitely join me in this habit.

131

Talk to Weirdos

Fast idea here in this mentoring message: chat with pirates, hang with misfits, and eat with oddballs.

You'll never grow in creativity, curiosity, enthusiasm, and wisdom having conversations with people who think, work, play and live just like you. If you're a baker, go befriend a gardener. If you're a teacher, go chill with a student. If you're an entrepreneur, go drink coffee with a tattoo artist and if you're a banker, go for a walk with a bagpiper. Such moves will make you rich.

Your growth lives not in the safe harbor but out in the blue ocean. And life's greatest risk is in taking no risks.

Go meet people who are different from you! Ask them questions, eat their food, learn from their lessons, and listen to their stories (because everyone we meet has a lesson to teach and a story to tell if we have the courage to be open to them).

The words attributed to Mark Twain speak to me deeply and I hope they'll do the same for you:

> Twenty years from now you will be more disappointed by the things that you didn't do than by the ones you did do. So throw off the bowlines. Sail away from the safe harbor. Catch the trade winds in your sails. Explore. Dream. Discover.

132

Dig Your Well
Before You're Thirsty

Business pundit Harvey Mackay wrote a classic called *Dig Your Well Before You're Thirsty*. In it, he shares how carefully he treats human connections. How well he prepares—when underpreparation yet overexpectation is common before every single meeting—going deep into learning about the background, interests, and achievements of the person he's about to greet.

This consistently causes gaspworthy responses from Harvey's new contact. And starts the relationship off at a uniquely excellent level.

Perhaps more essential, he advises people to "dig your well before you're thirsty." Develop mutually rewarding and profoundly fulfilling relationships not when you need something from someone but because the human connection will make their life and your life more prosperous.

People are smart and we can sniff insincerity a thousand miles away. Build your social community around being helpful, for the fun of the friendships and for the self-development that being around great people will bring you. Never do it because you're needy for a favor. Or hungry for an opportunity.

133

Don't Be a Servant to Your Phone

I hinted at this earlier, but I need to say it even louder: Don't use a phone in front of another human being you've committed to spend time with.

If I'm having lunch with someone who keeps watching their social media feed or checking their notifications while we're eating, I generally won't hang with them again. The behavior basically says their scrolling is more important than our conversation and they have better things to do than have a chat with me.

I was invited by the founders of a technology company to enjoy a dinner with them, as they wanted to use my content on their online education platform and have me represent their enterprise as their brand ambassador. All through the meal they checked their devices, took incoming calls, and watched short-form videos.

Their behavior was not only impolite, it showed me that they are addicts, unable to break free of their white screens for even an hour to interact with the person that they were hoping to have a partnership with.

Technology—intelligently used—is awesome. Properly leveraged, it allows for great things to happen and can enrich your relationships noticeably. Poorly handled, it can push people away and ruin your reputation.

So don't be a servant to your phone. Become a master of remaining present.

134

Make Others Feel Special

My life was transformed the day I stood in Nelson Mandela's prison cell on Robben Island. To walk through the limestone quarry where he was forced to do backbreaking labor for thirteen years and to see the propaganda office where censors would hide or alter letters from his family as a form of psychological torture and to then—finally—be allowed into a tiny cell (there wasn't even a bed in there) taught me what it means to turn pain into power and trouble into triumph.

One thing I learned on the visit was that Mr. Mandela invited a guard who treated him with courtesy and respect to his inauguration as president of South Africa—even though the statesman could have been angry and broken after twenty-seven years in confinement. Later he said, "As I walked out the door toward the gate that would lead to my freedom, I knew that if I didn't leave my bitterness behind, I'd still be in prison."

I share this to remind you that your job as a human is to make people become bigger in your presence. Small people try to show off, steal the spotlight, and act like the giant in the room. Usually, they do this to compensate for their sense of insecurity. Great souls make others feel great.

Make *everyone* you meet feel special. Give them sincere praise and recognize their gifts rather than condemning their faults. Live like this and you'll not only have more friends than you could ever imagine, but you'll experience a form of wealth well beyond anything money can buy.

Okay. We're at the end of the sixth form of wealth—having a strong and superb community of splendid people around you. You're doing great (I need to tell you that). And I'm grateful to be your mentor from afar. How about we head into the next form of wealth? You're going to find what you'll learn really valuable, as I walk you through the hidden treasures of a life abundant with adventure.

THE 7TH FORM OF WEALTH

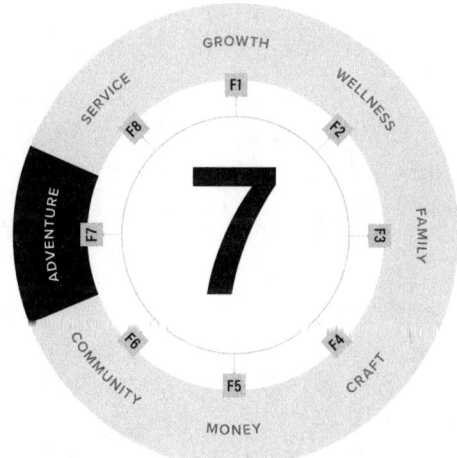

Adventure

The Joy Comes from Exploring Not Possessing Habit

*The important thing is not how many years in your life
but how much life in your years.*
—Edward Stieglitz, artist

The 7th Form of Wealth
Adventure | Quick Overview

Too many good people among us really do live the same year eighty times and call it a life. Getting up in the same way, thinking the same thoughts, being consumed by the same worries, walking to the same places, eating the same food, and seeing the same faces. We were not meant to live like this. Adventure is our ancestry and one of your biggest opportunities to lead your richest life.

Adding more wonder into your days—whether through actual travel to new sites or simply by reading a book that transports you to new lands or taking a novel route to work or embracing a fresh routine—really is a currency of vast beauty. Putting more awe, amazement, and excitement into your moments is a decision of wisdom that will make them into memories that you will treasure forever. Rich memories are more valuable than cash money, you know.

Yes, my always growing companion on this journey into true success and authentic prosperity, leading a life filled with passionate pursuits and enthusiastic explorations is very much a form of wealth. We are most awake when we are exploring and progressing, voyaging and daring. We are closest to our best selves when we are living audaciously instead of cautiously. "It is not death that one should fear but never having truly lived," said Marcus Aurelius, the glorious Roman emperor.

Our society values owning a lot of things instead of making a lot of life. Yet what's the point of having tons of possessions, storage lockers full of items and a gigantic home if you're mortgaging your happiness in the misguided pursuit of material things?

You, I humbly suggest, were not meant to live complacently. We are, as human beings, made to be nomads and produced to be pioneers. You come from a long lineage of people who scaled mighty mountains, discovered vast oceans, and traded the comfort of security for the sometimes uncertainty that enjoying a wildly alive life demands. Putting your personal passions ahead of your physical possessions will make sure that you never end up worldly rich but spiritually poor.

This form of wealth that I'm about to take you through is very much about bringing the curiosity, fascination, and sense of magic back into your hours—by flooding your days with more enriching experiences and astonishing instances. So you don't get to the end of your lifetime and realize you failed to live deeply.

Okay. We're onto the short roads of my mentoring time with you. I'm going to miss you when it's over. Anyway, let's not waste another second and head straight into the seventh form of wealth: adventure.

135

Find Your Invisible Panama

You might find this instruction, which I write to you from the energy of a big city, cool. Or maybe not (which is still cool with me).

This morning after an early workout (during which I worked up a nice sweat while listening to the audiobook *The Wizard and the Prophet*), I walked to get my coffee from a highly regarded café. I wound my way through the rain-soaked streets and past a soaring skyscraper that houses the offices and studios of a national broadcasting company.

It was still dark and there wasn't a soul in sight. I had the morning completely to myself! Then I heard rock music. Booming, actually. I thought it was from some sort of outdoor speaker that had been hung to entertain passersby. The song was "Panama" by Van Halen. I raised a fist, as one must do at a concert in the presence of rock royalty, thinking no one would see me.

As I continued to walk a few steps, it became clear that the sound was coming from a small minivan, a Dodge Caravan, actually. And the man inside had amped the song to please himself—and shake the ground, beneath his vehicle.

He smiled at me as our eyes met. He'd witnessed my fiercely enthusiastic fist-raising gesture. And seemed to be amused by what I had done.

The experience got me thinking. I'm not really sure, but my sense is that the man played the song as his elixir—to raise his spirits and create a few moments of glee before going into the concrete slab of a soul-crushing building to start his work.

And that got me thinking further about all the very good people on the planet today who betray their true passions to do labor that makes them miserable, uncreative, and sometimes even sick.

You might say, "But I have no choice—I have bills to pay."

Sorry. You *do* have a choice. You *do* have power. You could start a side venture like beginning an online video channel that shares your wisdom and educates viewers, or handcraft the novel you've always wished to write and then self-publish it online. Or open a pop-up shop to sell fantastic goods that light you up. Or create an invention that solves a big problem that you yourself have been struggling with. And if you don't know how to do this, then learn how to do this. I'm sure you can.

Another gentle piece of well-meaning advice that I'd like to reinforce: When you do what lights you up, you do your part to light up a brighter world for everyone. And when you push your magic into the universe, you model possibility for everybody.

Your life can be art, your job can be a gift and doing what is your heartsong is the very music that makes miracles real.

I'll leave you with the words I love from the esteemed author Herman Melville: "For as this appalling ocean surrounds the verdant land, so in the soul of man there lies one insular Tahiti, full of peace and joy, but encompassed by all the horrors of the half-known life."

136

Watch a Lot of Documentaries

I adore watching documentaries on lives superbly lived. Why? They are like getting intimate knowledge of how a great human being did what they did from an autobiography but in under an hour, if you get my drift?

From *Jiro Dreams of Sushi*, I learned profound insights on mastery; from *Salinger*, I discovered the history, habits, and hardships of a legendary writer. From *Amy*, I realized how dangerous being around dangerous people can be, and from *Good Fortune*, I was reminded that a life spent without making other lives better is a life poorly spent.

A good documentary allows you to enter into another person's existence. You can learn why they dreamed their dreams, how they got them done, the tricky traps of fortune, and the heroic joys of overcoming defeat. You can take new voyages to fresh places through documentaries. And upgrade your inspiration in the process.

The more you watch, the more ideas you'll get on the highest way for you to live. Then, filled with this knowledge, you can use each day as a platform to apply them. It won't always be easy, but I can promise you it will always be worth it.

137

Take a Digital Sabbatical

May I suggest that, to improve your lifestyle and also feel more alive, *at least* one day a week you go completely free of technology?

That means no phone, no social media, no chats, and no digital shopping for a full twenty-four-hour period. Every seven days.

To just live. To simply enjoy the basic, and often sensational, pleasures of your life. To be present (versus scattered) and centered (instead of stressed). To get lost in an unknown neighborhood or find a new bookstore. To test out a fresh food or walk barefoot in a secret park. To grow your love of the people around you who mean so much to you, and to maybe just get better at doing nothing.

Make a vow that at least one time a week from the moment you rise until the minute you sleep your devices will be turned off and placed in a drawer so they will be out of sight, so you can be awake. To wonder. To beauty. To nature. To the now.

Oh—there's another powerful method that I need to share with you to cut down on the digital distractions in your life that drain your sense of adventure. I call it The Two Phone Technique.

Have a main—fully loaded—phone that has all your social

media, news, weather, and other apps on it. Then invest in a second stripped-down phone that you carry when you are renewing or creating or doing anything that requires you to be completely focused. This way, you avoid being attached to and interrupted by your main one when you'd rather be doing something valuable—and essential.

Generations ago, once a week, people would take a day off (it was called a Sabbath). No work, no worries, no doing—more *being* was the name of the game here. The practice refreshed people's positivity and restored people's aliveness. My genuine hope is that you will do the same. To reconnect with the wonders that abound in our volatile yet still majestic world. To rekindle your childhood spark. And to refill your empty well.

138

Release The
Energy Vampires

We chatted a bit about this before. But I need to talk about it again as it's so incredibly important to you enjoying the journey of this blessing called your life. And because good mentoring requires regular reinforcing.

You can be happy or you can be with toxic people, but you will never, ever, ever be able to do both. All I'm saying is that if you want a strategy to transform your life almost instantly, say goodbye to all the people who make you feel bad.

If they are a family member, then see them less often. If they are a friend you've had for years but they are no longer growing with you and no longer vibing with you because they are negative or entitled or constantly complaining, then go ahead and keep loving them, but at a distance.

Yes, release the energy vampires and detox from the dream vultures. Free yourself from the happiness stealers. Life is just too short to spoil your good days by allowing pessimistic people to enter them.

139

Start a Garden

I once had a home that my family and I lived in for many years. I loved that place. Because of the way the sunrise would shine at the front of it through the trees, and the way we could light a fire in the winter and then watch the sun set through the forest behind the house every evening.

I liked the lightfall in the rooms, the fact that it was in a quiet area, and the reality that I could mountain bike late most afternoons in the woods nearby, after I'd finished my work. But one of the absolute best things about that place was its garden. I love flowers. They just fill me with contentedness and flood me with serenity. I found an expert to help me start the garden and I then began to care for it all spring and water the thing all summer.

"The first year it sleeps, the seconds year it creeps and the third year it leaps," I was told by the expert. And sure enough, at year three the lavender was lush, the coneflowers were luminous, and the tulips grew nearly as big as coconuts.

My parents came to visit one day just to sit in the back yard and stare at this natural miracle. "Who needs to go to a retreat?"

said my marvelous mother (yes, the one who took on a motorcycle gang—and won!).

Start a garden. Adding more adventure to your days doesn't mean you need to travel to foreign lands. Sometimes all you need to do is begin at your own home.

140

Become a Poet

To infuse your personal universe with less busyness, complexity, and negativity, my prayer is that you become a poet. It's a wonderful way to challenge your mind by creating an exploit on paper—and then beyond.

I'll explain what I mean, but first I'll offer you a poem that I wrote in my journal for you, at 5 AM. I know I'm not a very good poet, yet I honestly did my best:

The Quiet Promise

From birth to the end, there is a promise.
To befriend your hidden talents.
To delight in your highest visions.
To laugh at your human stumbles.
To know your soul's instructions.

From child to old.
The promise is betrayed.
In a swirl of daily rushing and endless doing.
As one does what adults are schooled to do.

Follow responsibility, fit in with polite society.
Prosper materially, to show a neighbor how rich you are.

The promise then feels unheard.
Eventually ignored.
A degraded humanity.
Stains on your birthright of possibility.
Chains on your destiny.
Through sleepwalking through a life.
Making one die invisibly.
And quietly.

To reclaim the dazzlement that you knew as a kid, I really do encourage you to become a poet. You'll probably be great, though you might not even know it! Not a bad one like me.

And I'm not talking about sitting down at a big wooden desk in a whitewashed cottage by the sea with pale blue shutters to write rhymes. (Although if that sounds inspiring to you, definitely do it.)

I just mean *live* again! By thinking often about all you need to become and taking the small, daily steps to make it all real so that by the time you're done, the ride will have been fun. And exciting. And fulfilling. And worth it.

Recall that most of the fears that limit us from our glory are fake dragons and false dreams. We create our own prison bars through faulty thinking and then spend our greatest years trapped in jails of our own making. Trust that there can be no progress without a few problems and no happiness without a few good fights.

Forget the need to please *everyone*. Care for the call of your soul first. Because you can't give to others what you don't have. And making your genius real sends a green light to all around you to do the same.

So, yes, be a poet. Express your artistry. Embrace what's risky. Live more dangerously. Look for more beauty. Watch more sunrises, pick more flowers, eat more pizza, hug more people, dare more freely, and count the stars that dot the dark sky. If they came out only once in a generation, you'd behold them. But because they are always there, you may not even appreciate them.

Yes. Be a who-cares-what-other-people-think poet. Not just on paper. But within your richest life.

141
—

Slow Everything Down

Join The Slow Movement. Many people are into slow cooking, slow eating, and slow working (being far more patient, thoughtful and careful as they perform their craft).

I recommend that you practice slow *living*. Accept fewer requests to do things you really don't want to do, buy less stuff, enjoy your days with fewer To Do's, make more time for interesting conversations, and pause to savor the obvious gifts of life most of us are so busy being busy that we miss. Busier is mostly never better.

Breathe more slowly. Chew more slowly. Walk more slowly. Talk more slowly. Think more slowly and feel more profoundly.

Slowing everything down—versus speeding everything up and living like your pants are on fire—doesn't mean you're lazy. It only means you're wise.

142

Go Ghost for a Year

I'll now offer a strange yet perhaps fascinating and, I promise you, powerful idea: for an entire year, go dark. Be hard to reach. Go ghost. Completely.

Yes, for twelve life-altering months, say no to most social invitations, refuse new friendship requests, stop shopping at stores, avoid going to restaurants, and pull back from the world.

Instead, enter the wilderness (of sorts), become a minimalist. Get monomaniacally focused, centered and grounded on what I call in my mentoring methodology The Vital Few.

> . . . Devote yourself to your personal growth and self-healing for a full year, understanding that the universe outside of you perfectly reflects the universe within. Get brilliant at meditating, visualizing, praying, journaling, and releasing the limitations blocking you from living your promise and realizing your potential.
>
> . . . Get into the fittest physical condition you've ever been in. Run or do push-ups, discover yoga or start surfing, get more fresh air and give yourself more sleep.
>
> . . . Read every book available in your field of expertise and practice your learnings for hours daily so you become so

knowledgeable, valuable, and excellent that no peer can touch you. And no problem will ever stop you.

... Restrict your spending, reduce your needs, and scale your savings so you battleproof yourself from any sudden financial emergency or a global economic catastrophe (and increase the peace of mind that comes with having no debt).

... Simplify your life and streamline your days by shedding all things that steal your joy and confuse your priorities.

... Enjoy the classics, study your heroes, listen to gorgeous music, eat natural food, consume clean water, withdraw from any addictions (scrolling, overworking, complaining and drinking might be good places to start), and take long walks in the woods, as often as you can.

... Forgive the ones whom you need to forgive, love the ones who deserve to be loved, and basically make yourself into the person you need to become to have the genuine fortune you currently most desire.

Yes, what I am requesting of you and even challenging you to do is to go ghost for twelve full months. In some place on the planet you've always wanted to visit. Or maybe go dark at your home. Make becoming your best your highest project for twelve months.

Then, once done, return to the world. Transformed. Born anew. Profoundly improved. Set to uplift us all.

143

Seek The Mysterious in Your Work

A very good way to elevate the wonder and quality of possibility in your life is to see the work you do as a doorway into new heavens of exploration. And higher orbits of excitement.

To relook at your work with the eyes of an artist and to dedicate yourself to pushing past boundaries, breaking fresh ground, and investing in novel things will not only significantly raise your inspiration, energy and personal bravery, it will shift your life from the mundane into the miraculous.

One of the snares we get caught in is repeating the way we've always worked. This is done to protect the success we've achieved and because we are afraid that innovating could cause a failure. Yet to operate in this way is to guarantee that you'll become bored, lifeless, and cynical.

Instead, pursue the unexpected. Try a seemingly weird style of productivity or a more unusual mode of doing what you do. Some might think you're kooky, yet it's the misfits and eccentrics who make all progress (and move the world ahead).

Famed artist Georg Baselitz radically changed the style he'd used for years when, in 1969, he started to paint and display his art upside down. Can you imagine that? Upside down!

He made this shift to "inverted painting" as he just wanted to do his own thing without the pressure of having to do what was expected by the art world.

You too can be this free. Your work can be a holy crusade—an enchanting odyssey into not only your finest creativity but toward your greatest self. Because the projects that scare you make you stronger. And only the people who push past their limits get to know how unlimited they really are.

144

Win The Memory Lottery

"Robin, I've come to the conclusion that too much money is a very bad thing," one of the world's wealthiest people told me as we walked by a river near a forest filled with wildflowers, deer and towering trees that must have been hundreds or even thousands of years old.

"Why?" I asked.

"Well, too much money is like a drug for extremely ambitious, driven, perfectionistic people like me. We keep on chasing it to make us feel like we're winning. But we aren't."

"Then what is winning to you?" I asked, as a fawn leapt by.

"Making more memories, not more money. When I get old, I want to enjoy thinking about all the special moments I've had with my family. On my deathbed I won't be able to take all the money I've made with me. I've never seen an armored truck at the end of a funeral procession on the way to a graveyard," the billionaire spoke softly.

Making more memories instead of chasing too much money. What a wise focus for us. At this time within our culture where too many people forget that freedom means so much more than long numbers on a net worth statement.

145

Do Something Scary Every Three Months

Quick chapter for you here. I once had a sailing instructor who was one of the most alive, funny, and interesting human beings I've ever met. His name was Bob. Special man. Cool dude.

On a long sail one summer's day, Bob shared a strategy that kept him young and energetic, and made sure he never lost the sparkle in his eyes (*never* lose the sparkle in *your* eyes). Every quarter he'd do something that scared him and every two years he'd commit to learning a new skill that reinvented him.

If you and I were on a sailboat together, I'd ask you carefully about all the things that you're not doing because they frighten you. Then I'd ask you to commit to accomplishing one, every three months. So you take back the power you gave to every one of those scary things.

And next I'd ask you to list major skills that you've always dreamed of learning. And I'd gently yet firmly ask you to promise me you'll work on mastering them. By working on them one by one, every two years.

Then I'd ask you a pretty gorgeous question that happy and terrific people often ask themselves: "When was the last time you did something for the first time?"

Finally, I'd ask you to help me set the sail. So we don't get lost at sea.

146
Pretend You're a Pirate

Speaking of the sea. I'd like you to pretend you're a pirate. Not a bad pirate, but a really good one (with nice teeth, decent manners and excellent habits).

Yes—I'm serious—to help you infuse your moments with the awesome experiences that make unforgettable memories—*be a little more dangerous.*

"Robin, what the heck are you talking about here?" you wonder. "Why are you encouraging me to become *dangerous*?"

Allow me to give you some examples of being slightly more of an outlaw than you currently are (unless you're already a major outlaw, in which case I recommend you skip this chapter and move ahead to the next).

- ... Ask your romantic partner to give you exactly what you want and your friends to give you precisely what you need.
- ... Ask for the best table at your favorite restaurant if you see it's available but the staff person is taking you to another one.
- ... Ask for the dessert that looks best in the bakery window instead of the one the baker is about to hand you. Take even more of a risk (oh how much life we waste for fear of being

rejected!) and ask for a dollop of chocolate sauce on it. I dare you.

... Ask for directions from a stranger who looks grumpy instead of from one who looks perky (and friendly).

... Ask the taxi driver to turn off the music because you don't like disco or not to chat on the phone with their therapist about their dramas. Because you're paying them to be working, not healing.

... Ask for an upgrade at a hotel ("would it be possible to put me into the penthouse, please?" is what a real pirate would say), a gigantic favor from a family member, and an extra scoop of ice cream at the ice cream store ("with more candy sprinkles than you've ever given, if you don't mind").

"No ask, no get" is a splendid mantra and "the only failure is the failure to try" is a superb autosuggestion. Success very much is a numbers game and not much happens if you always stay silent.

Being assertive need not be aggressive. Politeness mesmerizes, and all I really want is that you be even more brave instead of being too quiet.

Pirates get more bounty, live with a lot more color and, as far as I can tell, have a whole lot more fun.

147

Pursue Your Passions

Isn't it interesting that as we become adults we stop enjoying the pursuits that made us happy as kids? If we were having dinner together in my book-filled library, I'd ask you another top question: "What would the child you once were think of the grown-up you've become?"

I chatted with a tech-titan client the other day who said he was happiest in his life when he'd go on extremely long bike rides at least a few times a week. I asked him why he no longer does them. He invested in working with me because he's not very happy—and he admitted that the endurance rides made him so happy.

"Not sure," he admitted.

The luminary had allowed his heavyweight responsibilities and quest for elite achievement to distract him from one of the most precious treasures of a blissfully lived existence: having a ton of fun. He'd also forgotten that recreation re-creates us. Pursuing the passions that feed our enthusiasm and activate our joy makes us so much happier, creative, and productive and peaceful.

There's no sense in putting off the doing of your passions until you're too old to do anything about them. The majority of people are like that, sadly. They are rushing from place to place to keep up with their professional obligations, social commitments, and towering To Do Lists, ignoring the needs of their spirits in the process.

The weeks will slip into months and the months into years and the years into decades. Before they know it, it'll be too late to do anything about the fascinations they put off. Don't let that happen to you, my dear friend.

148

Less Mastery, More Mystery

I just watched a short video of a man who—in the interview—was referred to as "The King of Optimization." He was called this because for years he pushed himself physically and productively to reach the absolute limits of what was possible.

Interestingly, he noted he's now playing a different game. It's less about "life hacks" to get more done and more about slowing down the speed of life and having more adventures. Less about organizing his days at military-grade level and more about being free to wander (when he wants to) and rest (when he needs to).

I was happy to see this. Our civilization is going through a profound change. Many of us are asking ourselves some big questions: Who am I? What's my purpose? What does real success look like? How do I wish to be remembered?

Mastery *is* important. Most of us do want to realize our gifts and talents. And use our days productively (it's a supreme source of happiness to exercise our creativity and produce results that matter) while polishing personal skills that build our confidence, raise our resilience, and grow us into our higher versions of our finest selves. Yet as your mentor from afar who very much cares about you, I need to whisper this into your ear: *Forget not the magic.*

Don't be so busy being productive that you betray your soul's longings and become boring, uninteresting, and lifeless. Don't be so serious that you stop laughing at silliness. Don't be so driven that you forget how to be human.

Walk into The Mystery more often. Maybe just by—once in a while—spending entire days wandering and wasting time and simply *noticing* things. Or maybe you'll drive to a foreign town you've never had the time to visit in all these years of being too occupied, and allow yourself to get lost there. Or have a conversation with a shopkeeper about why they have spent a lifetime restoring old furniture. Or enjoy a conversation with a nonna who has made extraordinary pasta for sixty-five years (can I come?). Or with a farmer whose eyes glow when they speak of having the soil in their hands and their vegetables on another human being's dinner table.

Maybe these suggestions to go see more awe and wonder don't seem cool to you. That's fine—go do what seems right for you.

Far too many of us are chasing a definition of success that was sold to us by our parents, teachers, and society. We've followed their orders. Listened to their instructions. And where has it gotten us? Too often to unhappiness, stress and in some cases illness (mental or emotional or physical or spiritual).

Do not live your parents' life! Or your neighbor's way or by the method that influencers tell you you need to live to be liked, accepted, and popular. Live *your* life. It's all you have—and you're not going to get a second chance.

All I'm saying, as country music plays a little too loudly here at the farmhouse and the homesteaders off in the distance are harvesting their olives with traditional tools of a bygone era, is this: A truly wealthy life is not always about the pursuit of mastery. Mastery needs to be balanced with experiencing the miracles of the journey, more time in play, enjoying more magic, and leaning into the mystery.

149

Stop Salting Your Food Before You Taste It

I was in a restaurant with a friend when something sort of special happened. I'd like to tell you about it. As I think the lesson I learned will serve you very well.

We'd ordered and were speaking. The place was bustling, and the energy was awesome. When our lunch arrived, I picked up the pepper shaker and started shaking it all over my food. It's just what I do. (So I like pepper. Shoot me.)

My friend started laughing at my eccentric pepper-applying habit. Then he said, "Henry Ford would never hire you."

"What do you mean?" I asked as I chomped on my pepper-soaked food.

He explained that legend has it that the iconic tycoon would take prospective employees out to lunch to study them. He not only paid attention to how they treated the waiters (because that says a lot about one's character), he watched if they would salt and pepper their food before even tasting it.

The mythology goes that if someone salts and peppers their

meal before even testing it, it suggests three things about the person that makes them a bad hire:

Suggestion #1: The behavior disrespects the assumed skill of the chef and the hospitality of the host who has taken you there.

Suggestion #2: The person doing this makes decisions that are not based on any analysis whatsoever. Hmmm. Interesting.

Suggestion #3: The culprit doesn't have an open mind (and is set in their ways).

I smiled. And went more lightly on the pepper, while realizing that I'm pretty much unemployable.

Yet there is a wise life truth here when it comes to the seventh form of wealth that I want you to work on: Be not too deeply set in your ways if you seek to lead a fully inspired and deeply alive life. Keep an open mind (as it never hurts to question the beliefs you have always been sure are true), challenge your assumptions about what is possible for you to experience, and fight any limitations that are keeping your bigness small.

150

Happiness Is an Inside Job

So many good souls are trapped on the treadmill of telling themselves that they'll be happy and enjoy life's journey "when I."

. . . I'll be happy when I find the ideal love partner.

. . . I'll be happy when I'm in radiant health and have sculpted abs and a snow-white smile.

. . . I'll be happy when I get the right car or have a hot job.

. . . I'll be happy when I have tons of money and financial freedom.

. . . I'll be happy when the pace of change slows, the political, social and climate disruption stabilizes, and the messes on our planet subside.

Sorry, but not even one of these items will ever make and keep you happy—that's just an illusion sold to us by a society that in many ways has lost its way. They might bring you some short-term *pleasure* but that's different from *happiness*.

Only something inside of you can make you happy. Joyfulness is an internal state you create and a choice you make (by your daily thoughts, habits, behaviors, accomplishments, and adventures) instead of a thing that mystically happens some sunny morning when you find the right mate, house, job, or watch.

151

Do a Possessions Purge

Mess creates stress. And having too many things around us drains us of our energy, distracts us from enjoying the present moment, and wastes our money on stuff we don't need.

So do a purge. A gargantuan one!

Give away clothes you haven't worn in years, shoes you haven't used in months, and trinkets that seemed like a good idea to buy at the time but now seem as valuable as a fortune cookie to a clairvoyant.

The more you declutter, the more clutter you'll notice around you. Keep giving things away. Let go of all the mess. Clean sweep everything. Simplify!

Follow my suggestion and guess what you'll find? Space will be made for all-new levels of creativity. Your energy will accelerate and your precious feelings of personal freedom will take flight.

"The greatest wealth is to live content with little," instructed Plato. May we cherish his wisdom. Always.

152

My Top 10 Books on Leading a Life of Astonishment

Here are ten books that have assisted me in living a life of far less boredom, increased excitement, and a lot more wonder. I hope you'll read each one of them and then act on the ideas you learn (because information unapplied is worthless).

Into the Wild by Jon Krakauer
Small Graces by Kent Nerburn
The Little Prince by Antoine de Saint-Exupéry
Hope for the Flowers by Trina Paulus
Outsider by Brett Popplewell
The Giving Tree by Shel Silverstein
Endurance by Alfred Lansing
The Water in Between by Kevin Patterson
A Cook's Tour by Anthony Bourdain
My Last Supper by Melanie Dunea

Remember the importance of less scrolling and more reading, for a gorgeous (and honestly wealthy) life. And that most of the fears that stop us from living full on are nothing more than lies scared people have taught us.

153

Create an
Anti-Hero Scenario

Sometimes you need to shock yourself a little to make sure you never fall into a rut. To do this I'd like you to *mildly* terrify yourself by using a strategy from my methodology called The Anti-Hero Scenario. It's simple and it works beautifully.

Write a full page *not* about all the remarkable rewards that are coming to you by doing all I've been gently teaching you. Write instead about all the aggravation, frustration, and danger that will drown your life if you *don't* do what I've worked so carefully and devotedly to offer you.

- . . . Document all the dreams that will die, the fortunes you'll neglect, and the moments you'll miss by betraying your potential and getting stuck in your comfort zone.
- . . . Log the downhill trend your relationships will follow if you fail to keep your promises, open your heart, and present your real self to others.
- . . . Record the toxicity that will infect your Mindset, the pain that will invade your Heartset, the dis-ease that will degrade your Healthset, and the suffering that will stain

your Soulset if you neglect doing the things you must do to make your life what you and I know it deserves to be.

Yes. Get completely clear and a tiny bit scared about what will happen if you become not the victorious hero but the vicious villain of your lifetime. Frighten yourself (a little) into making the microchanges, the small triumphs, and the easy daily leaps that, when done consistently over time, will remake you into the human you've always wished you'd become.

154

Avoid The
Old Person Flaw

I very much respect elders. I really, really do.

They are—through so many decades of life—often the kindest, funniest, and most thoughtful people I meet.

And yet, I must also share that many carry a flaw: *they spend hours in conversation living in the past.*

- . . . speaking of exploits and adventures they did in their youth
- . . . offering anecdotes, tales of triumphs, and explorations that are ages old
- . . . talking in sensationally long monologues about the dragons they slayed, the mountains they climbed, and the feats they achieved

I'm not complaining. Simply reporting. In no way judging—just saying. It gets boring.

And as I see this phenomenon unfold, I realize that such good souls are *stuck*.

They've fallen into the trap of believing that their best days are behind them. They've lost a lot of their hope. They fail to see better times in a brighter future. Because the number of days ahead is far fewer than the days that have gone by.

And so, they cling to their stories. Recalling the special moments over and over and over.

Please be cautious about this. So you avoid doing it. And make what's coming even better. As you grow older.

155

Find Your Metaphorical Wolfgat

Part of what makes the increasing of adventure as you advance in your life so magical is the commitment and effort needed to realize your Project X (remember that concept from an earlier mentoring session in the craft section?), overcoming the challenges to express more of your native genius, and staying focused on your mighty mission. What I'm really trying to say today is that doing something fun and thrilling is so much more wonderful *when it's a reward for doing something hard.* And when the escape is the fruit of your labor.

There's an isolated little fishing village called Paternoster on the west coast of South Africa that I retreated to when I was writing different parts of *The 5AM Club*. This began a love affair with the place. It's ruggedly extraordinary and it has supremely down-to-earth people. Which brings me to Wolfgat, one of my favorite restaurants in the world.

This twenty-seat jewel is housed in a cottage, perched on a cliff over a barren Paternoster beach. Stylish music plays as the waves crash, and Wolfgat offers such special food that this off-the-beaten-path place was named the best restaurant on the planet.

Chef Kobus van der Merwe is a global leader in foraging (most ingredients for his dishes come from his nearby surroundings and his kitchen is stocked with indigenous plants) and a grandmaster of making simple yet exquisite wild food plates. He's been described as "a true renaissance man: physician, botanist, chef and poet."

Yesterday Elle and I had lunch there. The experience was soulful, astonishing and utterly unforgettable. I couldn't wipe the smile off my face for the first hour there. Seriously.

After weeks and weeks of working on this part of this book—and feeling creatively weary and spiritually empty—I took time off to travel to this oasis that brings me such joy, healing, and serenity.

All I'm saying is that life has a strange way of flying by all too fast. The adage "Too soon old, too late wise" speaks profound truth.

Find the spots on this wide planet that make you feel blessed to be alive. Find the spaces that cause your heart to flutter and your happiness to soar. When you work, work with devotion and when you play, do it with passion. And definitely do find your own metaphorical Wolfgat. Then go there. Before it's too late.

THE 8TH FORM OF WEALTH

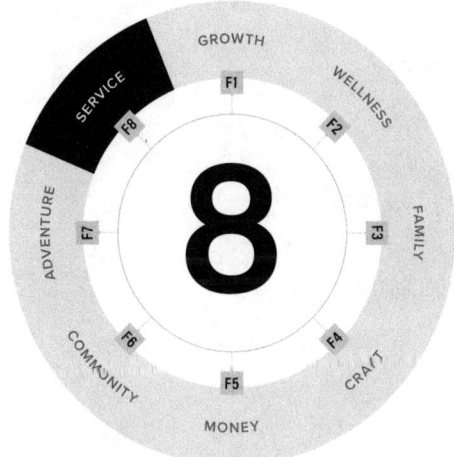

Service

The Life Is Short So Be Very Helpful Habit

In a gentle way you can shake the world.
—Mahatma Gandhi

The 8th Form of Wealth
Service | Quick Overview

Forget the bumper sticker that says, "The one who dies with the most toys wins." You just can't take your things with you when you go. So enjoy them, but definitely do not define who you are or measure your success by the possessions that you have. As you now know so well, material things are fleeting. They come and go. Trust that your human growth, your good health, your strong family life, your craft mastery, your rich social network, and your splendid adventures are the new status symbols of an honestly luxurious lifestyle.

Which brings me to you being your most helpful self. Service to others is an extraordinarily valuable currency. Being good to people makes you a wealthy person. This is not a popular belief. Yet it is a statement of truth. Your contribution matters. Your usefulness counts. Your impact is worth so much.

Few virtues will give you as much personal fulfillment and inner peace as having a positive impact on many. "To live in hearts we leave behind is not to die," wrote the poet Thomas Campbell.

To sincerely improve lives and to make a key difference are the habits of heroes and the legacy of legends. And one of the major areas anyone who wants to lead their richest life concentrates on upgrading, constantly.

Just to reinforce, I'm in no way saying there's anything wrong with making money, rising financially, and having marvelous material things. I've tried very hard since we first met to suggest that a gorgeous existence is all about maintaining a *balance* among all eight forms of wealth.

Okay. With this context, we need to start our journey together through the final form of wealth: service. So let us begin.

156

Find a Cause That's Bigger Than Yourself

Psychologist Abraham Maslow is famous for his hierarchy of human needs. If you haven't seen it, the framework looks like a pyramid. At the bottom are the most basic needs of human beings, which he refers to as "Physiological Needs" (such as food and shelter). Once these are satisfied, Maslow said we then become able to rise to steadily fulfil the next levels of necessities: our "Safety" needs (personal security, work, health and prosperity), then higher to our "Love and Belonging" needs and then up to "Esteem" needs, which are all about self-respect and the desire for recognition and status.

At the top of the popular framework is "Self-Actualization." Once all lower needs have been met, the thinking goes, we gain the strength, confidence, and personal armor to pursue the lofty and yet deeply important work of becoming all we are meant to be. To realize our potential. To live our gifts. To own our primal genius.

Here's the fascinating thing: just before Maslow died he decided to add one new level above self-actualization, at the peak of the pyramid. He called it "self-transcendence."

In other words, after living a full life, he realized that the highest hunger of you, me, and everyone else walking the planet today is to exist for something greater than ourselves. For a mission that transcends our self-centered needs. For a calling that leaves everyone we meet better than when we found them, and for a cause that makes some form of contribution. Yes, as human beings we are invisibly hardwired to serve. And as we do so—even in the tiniest of ways—we light ourselves up. While we bring light into the world.

Too few of us reflect on our main aim and central purpose until too much time has passed to do anything about it. My sincere hope is that you never allow this to happen to you.

157

Put Your Final Day First

"Life can only be understood backwards but it must be lived forwards," observed philosopher Søren Kierkegaard. How true.

It's only when we are near the end that we can connect the dots, spot the patterns and sense that *everything* that happened—even and especially the hard events—served a splendid purpose. And followed a sort of masterplan.

It was all soil for your growth, helping you learn the lessons you needed in order to grow into everything you were blessed to become in this lifetime.

My encouragement today? *Put your last day first.*

Yes, that's my wish for you now, as your endlessly encouraging and always enthusiastic long-distance mentor. Carve out some quiet time and, all alone, carefully consider the final day of your life. Imagine you're on your deathbed. See the faces of your loved ones. Assuming you lived truly, energetically, bravely, happily, and genuinely wealthily, what are they saying as they celebrate your magnificently well-lived life?

Think through the accomplishments you need to have achieved and which explorations you feel you needed to have taken for you to know—as you take your last few breaths—that you applied your sharper talents and promise well. Intimacy with your mortality is a powerful way to bring your vital few priorities into focus. And live to the point. As the eighteenth-century writer Samuel Johnson once wrote: "When a person knows they are to be hanged in a month it concentrates their mind wonderfully."

A confession: I used to read obituaries as part of my morning routine when I was a younger man. The discipline worked quite nicely to direct my hours to the pursuits that mattered most. Few things increase our commitment to stripping out what's trivial and doing what's essential as the threat of death. Sorry to say this yet I need to say it, to be of service to you.

In all the obituaries of lives wisely lived that I read, not even one said, "He died in his sleep surrounded by his lawyer, accountant and investment adviser."

No. Every single death notice of a human Earthwalk done with optimism and wonder, vitality and integrity, joy and serenity said, more or less, the same kind of thing:

> They died peacefully in their sleep at a very old age, surrounded by the coworkers who respected them, the neighbors who appreciated them, and the family that adored them. And they passed on with a soft smile on their face. Knowing they lived with authenticity, courage, creativity, and kindness.

May I enthusiastically ask you now: If such priorities will matter most at the end, why not have the courage to make them your primary focus now?

158

Memorize Alexander The Great's Last 3 Wishes

A famous legend holds that Alexander the Great, on his deathbed, gathered his league of generals and shared with them his three final wishes. They were:

That only the world's best doctors should carry his coffin.

That the vast economic wealth he'd accumulated over his lifetime (gold, precious stones, ornaments) should be scattered along the procession to the cemetery.

That his hands should hang outside of his coffin for all who gathered to view.

One of his top generals asked him to explain the reason for these three instructions. Here's how the revered ruler replied:

First, he stated that he wanted the finest doctors to carry the coffin so that all witnesses, and the population at large, would understand that even the greatest medicine available had no power to prevent a human being from dying.

Second, he wanted the streets to be littered with his gold and other forms of financial fortune so everyone in attendance would understand that money made on Earth remains on Earth after we die.

And finally, he said that he wanted his hands to hang outside the coffin so that his followers would know—and never forget—that we are born with nothing and die empty-handed.

May we memorize Alexander the Great's three final wishes deeply. And then apply them to our lives quickly. So we experience the wealth that money can't buy, immediately.

159

Lead Without a Title

Short message here. For almost thirty years I've traveled the planet (from London to Lagos, New York to Nairobi, Dubai to Durban, and Helsinki to Hong Kong), giving keynote presentations built around the idea that no matter where you live and no matter what you do, you can—if you choose—behave as a leader. Because leadership is simply the opposite of victimhood. And people operating as victims (by complaining, blaming, and waiting for conditions to get better rather than exercising their natural power to make them better) never, ever have a positive impact.

"Everyone can be great because everyone can serve. You don't have to have a college degree to serve. You don't have to make your subject and your verb agree to serve. You only need a heart full of grace. A soul generated by love," spoke Martin Luther King Jr., a hero of mine.

So go ahead. Lead at work even if you have no formal position or weighty job title. Lead at home, by encouraging, supporting, and cherishing your family (and being a rock in the storms). And lead in your community by behaving in a way that moves others to remember all they are meant to be.

160

Trust The Power of Not Caring

This might be strange advice yet here we go: *Care a lot but don't care too much.* That's what I'd say. And I'm not talking about being kind and treating people well. There, you do want to care too much.

I'm speaking of protecting your peace and working with reality in such a way that you're in the world but not really tied to the world. You're doing your best but holding on to whatever happens with a very light (versus tight) grip—trusting that the universe knows what it's doing and there's a wonderful reason for *everything* that's happening—even if you can't see the beautiful benefit in this very moment. Life unfolds not for your failure but always for your fortune, right?

Operate like this and you'll become a sort of modern-day spiritual master. Savoring the great seasons of your ride and trusting that in the mean ones your growth, bravery, and wisdom are forming. Once you've got the lessons that your highest self has needed, all hardship shall pass. And the better days will begin.

161

Your Heart Is Wiser Than Your Head

We are in an ongoing battle: between our Egoic Selves and our Heroic Selves. Between our birthright of freedom and the factory-installed programming of fear. Between the instructions our good hearts constantly (though quietly) send us and the relentless suggestions our noisy minds bark at us.

Your Egoic Self is not the real you. It's the part of you that's been created as you've gone through life and been told by all the influences around you how to think, what to say and how to live. It's the portion of you that has been formed by the hurts you've experienced, the disappointments you've endured, and the setbacks that you didn't know how to turn into strengths. Your ego is your shadow side. It's suspicious, scared, and sometimes selfish. And it works almost daily to sabotage you from being your finest.

Your Heroic Self? Well, that's the real you. It's rich with imagination insight, power, and love. It knows what you should do in every situation—for the benefit of *all* involved (not just yourself), is sure of your native greatness and is more undefeatable than our lower thinking can ever know. And this brilliant part of you understands that all of your heart's desires are your heart's desires because they are customized just for you—so you also have the ability to make them come true.

I guess what I'm saying is that although it's not "normal" to trust what your heart is telling you to do in this machine age, you really should. It's so much wiser than what reason is selling you. It would be good to start following it more.

162

Don't Let Another's Bad Day Ruin Yours

You get up early. The streets are still. The world is yours. If you get what I mean.

You do some exercise to bring your fire to life. Listen to some music, maybe make a coffee or enjoy some tea. Then you write in your journal about the things you're grateful for to introduce greater cheerfulness to your day and note a few lines to guide how you'll use the coming hours to bring you nearer to your vision of how it all needs to look at the very end.

Your morning routine has put you in a splendid mood. You're thinking positively, feeling super strong, and set to make the day you've been blessed with great. Then you meet another human.

Maybe it's within your home. Someone's woken up cranky and wants to invite you into their negativity. Maybe it's a fellow commuter on the train playing their video game too loud. Perhaps you walk into a bakery to pick up a cookie, greet the person behind the counter happily and they just stare at you, ask what you want and hand it to you rudely.

Look, just because so many others seem to be in a bad mood

much of the time doesn't mean you should let them ruin yours. Don't plug into their energy and get pulled into their orbit. You have the power to protect your peacefulness, honor your intentions for each day, and live life on your terms (rather than in a way that grumpy people silently wish you would). Because misery loves company. And dream stealers want you at their pity party.

163

Recite The Just Like Me Peacefulness Prayer

I once heard the mesmerizing monk Pema Chödrön speak of a prayer she performs when irritated or angered by another person.

She sits in silence, goes within, and then vows to forgive their bad behavior because "they are just like me."

I'm not sure if I've explained her exercise clearly or done justice to her wisdom.

All I'm saying is that she finds serenity in a moment of unhappiness by realizing that the bothersome thing another person is doing is something she likely also does.

And that connection with our common human weakness and communal imperfection provides her with tranquility. And causes her to relax, along with being of greater service to others.

It's ever so easy for all of us to sit on the summit of high judgment and the apex of self-righteousness on seeing another doing something we consider wrong.

Yet as we spend more time in reflection and awareness building, we often realize that we do the same thing.

Maybe the bad behavior of another of our brothers and sisters on this little planet looks slightly different from the thing that we do, yet the main idea here is that we too are regularly guilty of the very acts we find so troubling.

Given this, cut the wrongdoer some slack. Who knows what they've experienced and what they are going through. And then, be kind to yourself. You've gone through a lot too.

By engaging in the practice of praying for the power to forgive others because they are "just like me," we relax. We breathe. We ground. We open.

And then we arrive at the inner peace and outer positivity that helps us become more helpful to others.

164

See Solitude as The New Status Symbol

The celebrated sage Paramahansa Yogananda said these words: "Seclusion is the price of greatness." I absolutely love this.

Sometimes our egos and insecurities, fears and frustrations scream so loudly we can't hear what our souls are saying.

To carve out time for regular solitude is a holy act. To be alone and get supremely still is a sacred move. Why? Because in the quiet you'll begin to reconnect to your truest self. The one that is honest when others are lying. The one that is brave when others are retreating. The one that is excellent when others are coasting. The one that is loving when others may be mean.

Yes, my special friend (I'm going to miss mentoring you on these pages), go to secluded places far more often. Once there, consider what kind of a life you wish to construct. Reflect on what values you want to represent. And pray for the strength to live out the remainder of your days inspiring, encouraging, and enriching the lives of all around you.

Oh, last point here: you can't do your part to lead the world to a brighter place if you're always in it.

165

Apply The Kindness Always Motto

The writer and philosopher Leo Tolstoy (I'll tell you one of my favorite stories of his soon) observed that "Nothing can make our life, or the lives of other people, more beautiful than perpetual kindness."

Want to remove your worries and dissolve all troubles? Lose yourself in removing the worries and dissolving the troubles of others. By spreading kindness wherever you go.

One of the top regrets of people at the end of their lives is that they wish they had treated their family, friends, coworkers, and strangers with more graciousness, gentleness, and generosity.

When I was in my twenties, I was fortunate to have a mentor who taught me so much about what makes a rich life. He was impeccably well mannered, an example of excellence and a model of profound humility.

At our last meeting before he passed, when I asked this extraordinary person for his advice on what is most important to being fully alive, he simply said, "Be kind. Robin, *always* be kind."

I've never forgotten my mentor's wise words. I pray that you'll remember them too.

166

Doing a Good Thing
Is Never a Bad Thing

I was recently in a very poor part of the planet. It hurts my heart to see people struggling. Anyway, as I walked to the town I came across a couple of teenagers hanging out by a bridge.

"Sir, buy me a drink, please," the taller one said.

I continued to walk, then stopped. And turned around, going back to the kids.

"What do you mean by a drink?" I asked. "Not alcohol, right?"

"No, Sir, just something to drink. Or some food to eat. Please."

"Come with me," I replied. "Let's go to the grocery store."

And so the tall teenager and I walked to the food shop. It was a fifteen-minute trek and while we made our way to our destination I asked him about his family and about his dreams and of his worries.

Once at the grocery store, he stopped at the entrance. I think he was concerned that they wouldn't let him in, as his clothes were tattered and his shoes were torn.

"Come with me," I suggested politely.

He carefully followed me as we walked toward the deli.

"Do you like chicken?" I asked.

He nodded. "Very much."

"Today's my lucky day," he then mumbled.

"Five barbecue chicken thighs and five drumsticks and five large salads, please," I said to the woman behind the counter with a hairnet and thick glasses that made her eyes look wider than they were.

When I received the boxes over the counter, I handed them to the tall kid. He grinned a gargantuan smile.

"Thank you." Then he pushed his luck, as all young people should. "Can I get a soda?"

"No," was my answer. "I'll get you something healthy."

To his dismay, I picked up a few bottles of fresh orange juice and a carton of water. Then we headed to the checkout.

Once I paid for everything, he took the boxes and we walked into the late morning sunshine.

"Good luck with everything," was all I could think to say.

"Thank you," was his response as he walked away with a lightness to his step.

A bit later I met a friend who lives in the town. I asked if I'd done the right thing as I am not familiar with the culture and needed to know how things really worked there.

"You did fine, but now they'll ask you for food every time you walk by. You're a soft target now," he spoke, as he sipped a cup of coffee while standing on the street.

I went for lunch and then started to walk back to the place where I was staying. As I passed a grassy field, I saw the teenager. He was laughing loudly and playing football with his friends.

On seeing me, he called out, "Sir, thank you! Thank you for the food. And the juice. Thank you. Today was my lucky day! And my mates were very happy too!"

No asking for more. No pushing for extra. No soft target, anywhere in sight.

Just a grateful human being. Appreciating a small gesture. From someone who cared.

Look, I'm no guru and certainly no one special. But I will say this: *It's never a bad thing to do a good thing.*

In all these years of my sometimes hard life, almost everyone I've met has been inherently good. Sure, people have bad days (or decades) and we all have weaknesses (and wounds) that need to be worked on. Yet most people really have kind hearts and want to do well.

So whenever an opportunity for decency presents itself, go ahead and seize it. You might not have the chance again. And helping someone in need isn't just a gift you give to them. It's one you deliver upon yourself.

167

Reflect on The Lost Sovereigns Law

There's a time-honored law I invite you to consider: almost every single king, queen, president, prime minister, emperor, great military warrior, and iconic leader of history is no longer remembered. They were the titans of their time. The luminaries of their age, treated as gods by the masses and revered by millions. Now, shown to be mortal. And food for worms.

Today, you and I don't know 99 percent of them. We only remember a few of the truly monumental ones. The rest? Anonymous. Forgotten. Pretty much irrelevant. It's almost like they never even lived.

Gives us perspective, doesn't it? Even if we reach the pinnacle of success as our culture defines it, it's highly likely that aside from getting a long obituary and having family and a few friends give testimony at our funerals, no one will be thinking of us even a few months after we've passed.

Given this reality, your job is clear: Live *your* life. Do *your* dreams. Run *your* race. Stop living in a way designed to fit in, pacify all and avoid being rejected by the herd (which mostly leads you astray). No one remembers most of those heroes of history. So why take so seriously the need to march with the majority that you fail to have the life the wisest part of you wants?

168

Remember You Only Need Six Feet

Years ago, I used to share Leo Tolstoy's short story "How Much Land Does a Man Need?" within my leadership presentations. In it, a very greedy person becomes obsessed with acquiring more and more land in the place where he lives, to the point where he decides to move so he can possess even more.

He hears about a faraway region where the property is incredibly fertile and of a fantastic quality. So he travels there, bringing gifts for the leaders and charms the chief. On meeting them, the man explains that he wants as much land as possible. The chief tells him that he can have as much land as he can cover by foot in a single day.

The greedy property owner finds this deal a little odd but accepts the offer.

The chief says that the deal comes with only one condition: before sundown, the man must return to the point where he started, otherwise he will lose all the land he has covered during the day.

The man accepts and starts walking the land early the next morning. He walks briskly yet, in his avarice, picks up his pace so he can claim even more land. By midday, he is jogging so he can own even more property. By late afternoon he's running. On the first signs of the sun starting to go down in the sky, the man gets worried, fearing that he might not make it back to his starting point before sunset. And lose all he has gained.

He starts sprinting back to where he began, running faster and faster, as the sun sets lower and lower. Soon he's breathless and realizes that in his hunger for excess he has covered too much land. Yet he refuses to give up.

As the sun is close to moving beneath the horizon, the man sees the chief and his leaders on the hill waving to him and yelling at him to move even faster. So he does, eventually making it back to his starting place. The chief was delighted at the man's feat. He had accumulated a wonderful amount of fertile land. Terrific!

But blood was flowing from the man's mouth. His breathing had stopped. His eyes were shut.

A grave was then dug for the body. Six feet, from head to toe, was all the land the man truly needed.

My point? Helping is more valuable than acquiring. Giving is more fulfilling than taking. And being useful is more satisfying than collecting. One of the things I've observed in the lives of history's greatest souls is that each and every one of them had reached such a high level of consciousness that their dedication to becoming of service was far in excess of any desire to have possessions.

I went to Mother Teresa's mission in Calcutta on one trip and, after being led through various rooms, was walked up to the place where she'd sleep each night. It was *stunning* how few things this woman—who was revered by the world and beneficial to millions—owned. A total minimalist. Just an austere bed, spartan desk and not much else. Empty bedroom. Rich heart. Good spirit.

Mahatma Gandhi, another master of the ascetic lifestyle, had *only six* belongings at his deathbed, including his steel-framed glasses, a bowl, a plate, sandals, and his trusted pocket watch.

Material possessions simply held no attraction for him. He had arrived—through meditation, prayer, fasting, and working toward the freedom of his fellow citizens—at a state of being where his calling to serve gave him far more satisfaction than the showboating of a flashy car, the sporting of an expensive watch, and the owning of a home in a chic neighborhood could ever provide.

Again, do what's best for you. That's what I most want for you. But also know that real happiness, peace, and lasting personal freedom come from being a blessing to others and doing good things, while you travel through your days. And that someday in the oh-so-distant future all you'll need is six feet of soil.

169

Start a Love Revolution

A favor to ask of you if you're in the mood, ready to hear me and willing to do something that I think will considerably lift your sense of living with a passionate purpose: begin a love movement. Yes, a movement. By taking the first step.

Mahatma Gandhi's salt march, which grew into an uprising of millions that played a giant role in nonviolently freeing his nation from foreign domination, started with him taking one step. Alone. Then the second person joined, then a few more, then tens of his brothers and sisters of his country, then thousands and eventually everyone got involved with his originally crazy dream.

Rosa Parks wouldn't go to the back of the public bus designated for people with darker skin during the sad days of racial segregation. The driver told the seamstress that he'd have her arrested if she didn't do what she was told. "You may do that," she replied softly and with deep dignity. Her act of defiance led to a boycott of buses, which led to marches and protests, which ignited the Civil Rights Movement.

I want you to begin your own revolution. Yes, I really do! One based on love. (Guitar virtuoso Jimi Hendrix said, "When the power of love overcomes the love of power, the world will know peace.") And on the reminding of others to be more caring, respectful, polite, cheerful and endlessly forgiving, start small. Take little steps on your march. Make some symbolic gesture to attract more followers. And don't stop until you've fulfilled your mission. To change the world.

170

The High Road Is The Best Road

This morning, I was fed a short video where the social media influencer yelled, "Put yourself first or else you're a loser who will be taken advantage of."

Yesterday, I heard a top pundit share that he measured his success by how many people will attend his funeral.

Last week, I heard a leader talk about the nature of worldly power and the moves to make to snatch it from others, manipulate those you deal with, and reach the mountaintop of having it all.

Look—and I'd like to be clear—the great thing about a human life is we each get to have our own opinions. And I very much respect the right to free speech.

Yet I just see the universe ever so differently from so many. I guess you do too. That's why we vibe, right?

And I need to add my views to the conversation so you can consider them here, then form your own conclusions and find a truth that fits best for you.

So here I go . . .

. . . A strong, wise, great human being is one who cares deeply about the welfare of others. Of course, be not a doormat. For sure, if you allow people to take advantage of you, some will do so. That's obvious, so don't be naive, please. Yet I don't think that making it all about you will ever bring you the self-honor, happiness, and sense of serenity I know you seek. If you're good and someone takes from you, you're the victor—not them. Because you got to be good.

And ...

... Why does it matter how many people show up at your funeral? You'll be dead. What if no one shows up to mine? Who cares? Why is this a metric of success? My guess is that Vincent van Gogh died alone. Does that make his life unsuccessful? No, it was *remarkable*. To me, the man is a hero. What of the gardener or the gravedigger who lives quietly and with intense integrity, doing their work with dignity—and living with civility, wisdom, compassion and honor—who leaves the Earth with only a few at their funeral? Winners in my book. Absolute champs.

And ...

... Why does being powerful all too often mean stepping on others so you can rise? Isn't that hard on your heart and supremely bad for your soul? Is it just me or do you feel me? Isn't being honestly powerful all about lifting others up versus tearing people down? And helping people own their giftedness instead of advertising loudly about yours? And being a shining light on this planet with far too many shadows?

I just don't think you'll get all you want following the kind of advice those well-meaning gurus are offering. Instead, I suggest you become sure of these not-so-normal truths:

... Caring is cool.

... Politeness is hip.

... Reliability is hot.

... Humility is groovy.

... Frugality is sexy.
... Patience is potent.
... Selflessness is sensational.

I'll end with a precious story on this point about the importance of always taking the high road to an excellent, joyful, and *really* wealthy life.

Spanish athlete Iván Fernández Anaya was running second in a cross-country race in the Navarre region of northern Spain in 2012.

In the lead was top runner Abel Mutai, who had won the bronze medal at the London Olympic Games. Incredibly, Mutai—who was certain to win—stopped ten meters before the finish line, mistakenly believing he had crossed the line.

Rather than speeding past the leader for a clear victory, Fernández Anaya stopped and encouraged his confused competitor to keep running so he could claim his well-earned prize.

"I didn't deserve to win," observed the twenty-four-year-old Spanish athlete. "He was the rightful winner. He created a gap I couldn't have closed if he hadn't made a mistake."

That kind of character and selflessness is a pleasure to witness. It's sort of magical.

Let's celebrate the high road—and always head up to it.

171

Eat Your Last Supper Today

To add more meaning to your days, I recommend that you define your last supper. And then go eat it.

On the weekend that just ended, Elle and I were in Rome. On a trip, I prefer to eat a wonderful lunch and then have little to no dinner. This makes for a really fun day and a healthy, quiet evening (that promotes deep sleep). This way of eating also easily allows me to be up early the next morning to pray, meditate, exercise, journal, and read—which pretty much guarantees that the next day is another good day, if that makes sense to you.

We invited two of our friends to join us for lunch at one of my favorite restaurants. It's located close to Campo de' Fiori—a square where the legendary sixteenth-century thinker Giordano Bruno was burned alive for spreading revolutionary ideas. But that's another story that I'm saving to tell you, maybe if we get to meet in person sometime in the future (I'd like that).

We all ate the small-plated Roman delicacies. Oh, that burrata! It's an Italian cow's milk cheese that's formed from cream and mozzarella. It contains Stracciatella, which is a creamy, gooey, marvelously textured morsel of heaven. Quite divine. Exceptionally simple.

About two hours into what would become a four-hour meal

rich with laughter, deep talk and light chat, I asked the table, "What would you eat for your last meal?" I thought it was an interesting question to stimulate fascinating conversation.

My friend—who is an iconic DJ—immediately leapt into action, speaking of his favorite pasta, meat grilled on an open fire and the side plates he'd definitely enjoy.

Each of us had our fun. We covered a lot of food. When my turn came, I admitted I'd eat my dessert first (fresh ricotta cheese with raw honey drizzled delicately over it, please).

"What's your point here, Robin?" you wonder of your endlessly dedicated yet aging mentor.

"Easy," I'd gently reply. "The more you can remember the shortness of life and reconnect with your mortality—in a culture of being nonstop busy—the more power you'll have to say no to any invitation that doesn't really get you closer to where you want to be in the twilight of your lifetime. And the more strength you'll have to choose only those essential exploits and key opportunities that will get you to a place called amazing."

You can start by defining your final meal. And then fully enjoying it. Tonight.

172
—
Do Three Anonymous Acts of Goodness

Today, go out into our jaded, crisis-filled, and all-too-often selfish world and do three basic yet beautiful acts of humanity for three people who won't even know that it was you (anonymous generosity is the only type that means anything). Anne Frank wrote in her diary, "No one has ever become poor by giving." And writer Neil Gaiman said, "I hope you will dream dangerously and outrageously, that you'll make something that didn't exist before and that you will always be kind."

I'm not sure what three acts of goodness will most speak to you and which three you'll make the time to do this day. What I do know, though, is that decency has a domino effect, moving its receivers to be more caring as they advance through their hours. Yes, *you* really can improve the world. One person at a time.

I recently had a conversation at a Barcelona hotel with an always smiling doorman named Alberto. I mentioned that, by his usual positivity, if he left one hundred guests and passersby a day better than he found them, after five days he will have influenced and uplifted five hundred humans. I continued: "Alberto, that's two thousand a month and twenty-four thousand people in a year." He was silent. He looked up at the sky.

I would not stop, adding, "After ten years your goodness and grace will have touched nearly a quarter of a million people." Tears began to fill Alberto's big blue eyes.

Right there. Straight in front of me. On that elegant street in Barcelona.

Definitely think about this: being good to just three people a day means you will uplift ninety human beings in one month, one thousand and eighty in one year, ten thousand eight hundred in a decade, and almost one million people by living the normal lifespan (I hope you'll live far longer, though).

For sure, you can make that magnificent a difference. In many ways, though you may not know it, you already do.

173

You Matter Much More Than You Know

No one alive right now, in this very moment, is unnecessary. Each of us has talent, wonder, and astonishing powers within us. *Everyone matters.* Everyone has an impact on the world. And yes, that does very, very, very much mean you.

Our society places billionaires, sports stars, and celebrities on a pedestal. Many travel in motorcades, receive VIP treatment, and are greeted with overflowing crowds of admirers seeking selfies everywhere they go. Yet what about the sensationalism of the single parent working three jobs to put food on the family table and even, amidst the struggle, keeps a smile on their face, always staying a great example to their children?

Or how about the librarian, teacher, nursing home assistant, or street cleaner who works quietly, for the benefit of many, who receives no fame, fortune, or applause yet softly influences people's lives?

Should we not put their names in lights, seek their autographs, cheer at their efforts, and erect towering monuments to cherish their commitments?

All I'm saying is that we live in a period that mostly reveres the wrong things.

And that brings me back to you again. I'm not sure where you are on your life's process—whether you're at the summit or in the valley. But I do very much wish to remind you—intensely—that you do have magic within you, potential that needs to be realized, and a very real ability to impact humanity in a big, bold way. Or maybe simply in a tiny fashion, which is certainly just as valuable.

174

Have a Living Funeral

It's such a waste to have people speak of your conviction, achievements, and courage after you're dead.

You'll be six feet under or a pile of dust in an urn above a fireplace, so you won't be able to hear their tributes.

My suggested solution? Have a living funeral. Yes. I'm not kidding. *A living funeral.*

Schedule a time. Send out the invitations. Buy the cake (chocolate would be best). Maybe put fresh daisies on it (as weird as that would look).

Tell those you love of your experiment. That you wish to live like you're dying. That you are excited to exist more vividly, creatively, and enthusiastically—by performing this ritual to remind yourself that life passes in a blink.

Let your loved ones know that you need to pretend you're dead. To remind you of life, in all its fragile glory and delicate majesty.

Then explain that you want to bring together the people most important to you. To hear what they think is best about you. To tell them how you feel about them. For you to speak of the lessons you've learned, the trials you've endured and the triumphs you've enjoyed. To talk of love and how much those gathered mean to you, thanking each of them for the blessings they have given you.

Makes me think of a story I studied while I was writing *The Monk Who Sold His Ferrari*, oh-so-many years ago. There was once a great maharajah who had a most curious morning practice: He'd enact his own funeral—complete with music and flowers. And all the while, he'd chant, "I have lived richly and passionately, wonderfully and helpfully."

When I asked my beloved father why this man would run this routine—at every sunrise—my father replied with a wise smile: "Robin, that's easy. This man has developed a ritual to remind himself at the beginning of each day that this day could be his last. The maharajah developed this method to connect him to his mortality. And to remind him that this day could be his final one, so he'd live it completely and on his own terms."

Yes. Have a living funeral. It just might be your new birth day.

175

Live Fully So You Can Die Empty

I'm going to miss you. Thank you for allowing me to be of service to you, as you create a life filled with real riches and genuine wealth—one I'm sure you'll be very proud of at the end.

I'm at the old farmhouse as I write you this last message. I feel most grateful for my time with you. It's a sort of cold morning. A sweet country song plays. The birds sing and my weary eyes see a mist floating above the hills on the distance, beyond the olive grove. My heart tells me great gifts are coming to you and your future looks oh-so-blazingly bright. Congratulations. You deserve the best of everything, my special long-distance friend.

I won't take up much more of your time. I do hope our journey together has left you inspired, enriched, and absolutely dedicated to applying all I've humbly offered you, so it forms a part of your days. And becomes your new way of life.

What I most wish for you can be said quite simply though: *Live fully so you can die empty.*

Makes me think of what George Bernard Shaw once wrote:

This is the true joy in life, being used for a purpose recognized by yourself as a mighty one. Being a force of nature instead of a feverish, selfish little clod of ailments and grievances, complaining that the world will not devote itself to making you happy. I want to be thoroughly used up when I die, for the harder I work the more I live. I rejoice in life for its own sake. Life is no "brief candle" for me. It is a sort of splendid torch which I have got hold of for the moment, and I want to make it burn as brightly as possible before handing it on to future generations.

Thanks again for spending time with me in my messy writing room—along with my little dog SuperChum (who's right next to me now, waiting for me to take her for a walk)—as well as on my travels across this ultimately beautiful, exceptional, and completely-worth-saving planet. I do hope to meet you sometime, someplace, somewhere, to continue our conversation. About the wealth money can't buy.

Stay great, good soul. Continue believing in your dreams and being your own biggest fan. What's ahead for you is wonderful. And, don't worry... though I may not be next to you, I'll be watching you grow, prosper, and experience your richest life, as your mentor from afar.

Join *The Wealth Money Can't Buy* Movement

Unite with other people growing their richest lives and making a difference in the world by creating a short video or photo of you experiencing the wealth money can't buy. The best ones will be posted online.

Ideas include you . . .

　. . . performing your morning routine
　. . . walking in the beauty of nature
　. . . delighting in special moments with your family
　. . . engaging in a passion that inspires you
　. . . overcoming a deep challenge
　. . . enjoying a wonderful meal
　. . . producing great work through your craft
　. . . conquering a fear by taking a risk
　. . . traveling to a place you love
　. . . making a positive difference

To share your video, access excellent learning resources and to join the movement of people just like you who are dedicated to leading their finest lives, go to **thewealthmoneycantbuy.com**.

Fuel Your Rise by Reading All of Robin Sharma's Worldwide Bestsellers

Whether you're at your mountaintop of world-class or just starting your climb, reading is one of the master habits of true success and lasting happiness.

So here's a complete list of the author's massively popular books to support your ascent into your richest life:

[ ] *The Everyday Hero Manifesto*
[ ] *The 5AM Club*
[ ] *The Monk Who Sold His Ferrari*
[ ] *The Leader Who Had No Title*
[ ] *The Greatness Guide*
[ ] *The Greatness Guide, Book 2*
[ ] *Who Will Cry When You Die?*
[ ] *Leadership Wisdom from The Monk Who Sold His Ferrari*
[ ] *Family Wisdom from The Monk Who Sold His Ferrari*
[ ] *Discover Your Destiny with The Monk Who Sold His Ferrari*
[ ] *The Secret Letters of The Monk Who Sold His Ferrari*
[ ] *The Mastery Manual*
[ ] *The Little Black Book for Stunning Success*
[ ] *The Saint, The Surfer, and The CEO*

If you'd like free access to *The Wealth Money Can't Buy* online assessment and a complete video masterclass of living at your peak, get it at **thewealthmoneycantbuy.com**.

Activate Your Positivity. Maximize Your Productivity. Serve The World.

A playbook for leading your field, producing mastery, and living beautifully. Available everywhere good books are sold.

Own Your Morning.
Elevate Your Life.

The book that has helped millions of people start their days strong, increase their productivity, and experience their highest lives.

More Transformational Companions for Your Growth Journey

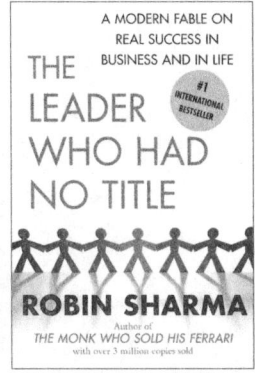

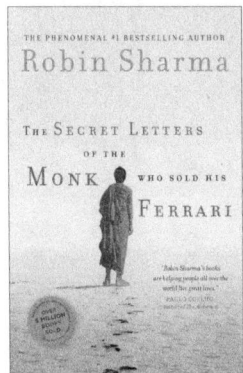
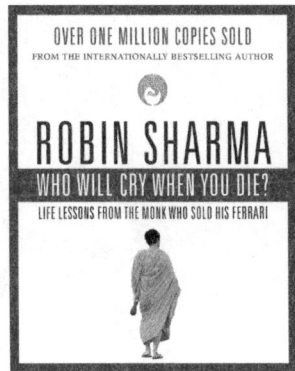

Read. Learn. Grow. Prosper.

About The Author

Robin Sharma is a globally respected humanitarian and the founder of a not-for-profit venture that helps children in need lead better lives. He has a particularly strong focus in ensuring kids suffering from leprosy rise.

Widely considered one of the world's top leadership experts, as well as an icon in the field of personal mastery, this pathblazer's clients include many Fortune 100 companies, famed billionaires, professional sports superstars, music legends, and members of royalty.

Organizations that have engaged Robin Sharma as a keynote speaker at their conferences to help them build employees who lead without a title, produce exceptional work, and master change in these complex times include Nike, FedEx, Microsoft, Unilever, Expedia, GE, HP, Starbucks, PwC, IBM Watson, Yale University, and YPO.

The author's #1 phenomenal bestsellers, such as *The 5AM Club*, *The Everyday Hero Manifesto*, *The Monk Who Sold His Ferrari*, *The Greatness Guide*, and *The Leader Who Had No Title*, have sold millions of copies in more than ninety-two languages and dialects, making him one of the most influential writers alive today.

To inquire about Robin Sharma's availability for your next convention, visit robinsharma.com/speaking.

To keep in touch with Robin, visit robinsharma.com and the following social media platforms: